A Bite-Size. .... DUUR

China: Engage!

Avoid The New Cold War

Vince Cable

Cover by
Dean Stockton

Published by Bite-Sized Books Ltd 2020
©Vince Cable 2020

BITE-SIZED
BOOKS

Bite-Sized Books Ltd Cleeve Road, Goring RG8 9BJ UK
information@bite-sizedbooks.com
**Registered in the UK. Company Registration
No: 9395379**

ISBN: 9798696318912

China: Engage! Reviews

Vince Cable's *China: Engage! Avoid the New Cold War* is free of jargon, full of evidence, and confronts the lazy assumptions that have characterised so much thinking about China for so long. Read this book.

Amol Rajan, BBC's Media Editor

Sir Vince Cable's China; Engage! is extremely well informed, balanced, easy to read and thought provoking. It is also absolutely relevant to policy in the UK and the USA and to the global financial markets.

Zhenbo Hou, BlueBay Asset Management

This is a splendid and most timely intervention. Cable has written a powerful book on a subject which is of enormous importance to the future of the UK and the world. In 2020 the UK flipped and fell victim to Sinophobia. We were transported back to the cold war. Cliches and prejudice usurped thinking and understanding. China was equated with the Soviet Union. Nothing could be further from the truth. The latter was an abject failure, China already has the largest economy in the world. Cable has clearly given a lot of thought to the question of China. As he argues, it is here to stay and will be at the heart of humanity's future for the next century and beyond. Far from being the incarnation of all evil, there is much that is hugely positive about China's rise. Read this book. You will be much the wiser about the world.

Martin Jacques, author, 'When China Rules the World'.

Contents

The Author

Vince Cable was MP for Twickenham for 20 years, retiring in 2019. He was Secretary of State for Business Innovation and Skills and President of the Board of Trade in the Coalition government from 2010-15.

Before entering parliament he had an extensive career in government, international organisations, universities and business, latterly as Chief Economist of Shell.

He has enjoyed Visiting Professorships at the LSE, Nottingham, Sheffield and St Mary's and Birmingham City Universities.

He is the author of many papers and including several books: *The Storm; After the Storm; Free Radical,* a memoir; *Globalisation and Global Governance;* and a novel, *Open Arms.* His latest book, *Money and Power* appears in February 2021 (Atlantic Press)

Chapter 1

Overview

Anyone doing business with China will have been shocked by the speed with which political and economic relations with Western, and some other, countries-like India – have deteriorated in 2020, but especially the USA and the UK. A crucial issue for the future is whether this is a passing phase, caused by temporary shocks like the Pandemic and by the personalities of leaders in China and the USA. Alternatively, this could be the beginning of a new Cold War characterised by prolonged hostility on several levels, especially the economic.

China is, by some way, the world's largest exporter of goods. Its products are embedded in world trade and form an integral part of global supply chains. Its imports are now the main influence on many commodity markets. Chinese companies' investment overseas and overseas investment in China have become hugely significant in international business. China matches in many areas, and in some areas leads, the US in technological capability. A key question is whether flows of trade, investment and technology are now at risk of serious disruption.

I shall try in this short book to identify the fundamental drivers of this emerging conflict.. The first is that the USA is being overhauled by China as the undisputed economic superpower. With that success comes great influence, political and economic, including the power to set the norms and standards for technology and business. In the United States, particularly, and also in Europe, the sense of China as a competitive threat is overtaking the dominant view of the last half-century which saw China mainly as an economic opportunity.

The second is that China's emergence is a challenging to the orthodox view-at least, since the collapse of the Soviet empire – that the only model which works is a Western-style system of market capitalism and liberal democracy. China has evolved an apparently successful form of 'state capitalism' backed by one-party, authoritarian – but competent and stable- government built around sophisticated surveillance. China is different from and not converging towards Western norms. The big question for the future is whether the two systems can coexist and cooperate. Pessimists are preparing for a new Cold War (or even a hot one).

Wise companies and governments will be thinking of different scenarios and how to respond to them. The view I take in this book is that China will continue to power ahead, economically and technologically. China will not go away. It will be a dominant player in some industries, technologies and in some parts of the world. My assessment is that, overall, the talk of Chinese 'expansionism' is exaggerated. And while growing Chinese influence may be uncomfortable we have to learn to live with it. China will also be an essential partner in tackling some global issues like climate change, economic coordination and the management of infectious diseases. It will continue to offer big business opportunities. The current rush to take sides in a new Cold War is unwise and dangerous.

Chapter 2.

China: the New Economic Superpower

Is China No2 or No 1 in economic size?

This seems a simple question of fact but isn't. In population terms, there are around 1.4 billion Chinese, slightly ahead of India (1.3 billion) though India will soon overtake it. The USA has with 330 million the third biggest population.

The area of dispute is over the size of GDP: in effect, the size of the market. It is usually asserted as a matter of fact that China now has the world's second highest GDP after the USA, and might catch up in a decade or so. That is almost certainly wrong. Let me explain why.

There is some argument as to how reliable Chinese statistics are, though they have been given a clean bill of health by the main financial institutions: the IMF and World Bank. On the assumption that the numbers are believable, in 2019 America posted an estimated $21.4 trillion worth of goods and services while China's GDP was worth $14 trillion converted into dollars from yuan at the average market exchange rate in 2019 (close to 7 to the dollar). So far, so good.

But 7 yuan (now, officially, called the renminbi) can buy a lot more in China than a dollar can buy in the USA. This difference in price levels has led to the calculation of Purchasing Power Parity (PPP) GDP as a truer measure of economic size. The IMF, the World Bank and the UN use PPP measures and they show the local Chinese currency as substantially undervalued. The IMF has GDP at $27.3 trillion and the World Bank, after some recent revisions, at around $24 trillion. Which estimate we choose explains whether China overtook the USA in 2014 or 2016. But the conclusion is clear: on a meaningful definition of economic size, China is undisputed No 1.

China's 40 years of Rapid Growth

The figures above give us a snapshot at one point in time. What matters, in the long run, is the trend in growth. Compounding big differences in growth rates exponentially over long periods of time makes a huge difference.

Back in 1980 when the Chinese leader, Deng Xiaoping, was starting the process of opening the Chinese economy, the US economy was almost ten times bigger (22% of world GDP versus 2.3%). What has happened since is that China powered ahead at double-digit growth while the USA, like other Western countries, progressed at a more sedate 2 to 3% p.a.

Then, the financial crisis a decade ago was a key inflection point, producing recession followed by slow growth in the US (Japan and Europe) while China enjoyed a spurt of growth powered by large-scale infrastructure spending. In recent years, China has slowed from double-digit growth to a more moderate level of around 6% pa while the USA has averaged around 2%pa.

Now, with the pandemic, we face a new inflection point. China is recovering economically after a ruthless lockdown and is expected to grow a little, maybe 1 to 3%, in 2020 while the US is facing a deep and painful contraction of up to 10% of GDP. The gap between China and the USA is widening, with the USA being left further behind.

But why should we believe the Chinese numbers?

After all, the Communist Party is in charge and we learned that in the USSR and Eastern Europe all those growth and production figures were a work of fiction. Factory managers cheated to meet their planning targets. Quality was dire. But China isn't remotely like the USSR in economic terms (politics is a different matter). It is a capitalist economy with highly competitive markets and global benchmarks. Its leading economic officials, especially those in the Central Bank, are regarded as highly competent technocrats. If there has been cheating it has been to understate progress so that China can continue to enjoy the privileges of being regarded as a developing country in the WTO and World Bank. Foreign analysts crawl over Chinese data and there is no serious suggestion of systematic inflation of Chinese growth. Hard, verifiable, data like electricity consumption and freight traffic gives support to the official numbers.

But can this juggernaut continue to power ahead? There are two alternative views. One is that China is running out of steam. It has, in addition to a legacy of old, inefficient industries and incompetent Communist managers, many of the problems of a more sophisticated, advanced, capitalist country, like an ageing population, a declining labour force and high debt levels. It may be entering what is called the 'middle income trap' resulting in a ceiling to rapid growth.

The other view is that China has still a long way to go to catch up with developed country living standards and has most of the elements needed for rapid growth until it gets there. These optimists say that Western commentators have consistently underestimated China's ability to adapt, innovate, reform and develop and are doing so again.

I will look at both sides of the argument.

Ageing: Is China Old Before Its Time?

The more negative view of Chinese growth has one powerful piece of evidence: demography. China is no longer a country with vast reserves of cheap labour from the poor, rural, interior who provided the working population for China's export industries and for its vast infrastructure projects. A combination

8

of rapid economic growth and a low birth rate, the legacy of the 'one child' policy, has meant that China is hitting limits to its labour force and is rapidly ageing, like Japan before it.

The working population is now just under 900 million and that number has been falling steadily for the last eight years from a peak of 941 million in 2012. Projections suggest it could fall by another 100 million by 2035. The critical factor is the very low birth rate. China was worried about excess population in the 1970's and brought in a 'one child' policy with strong disincentives for larger families, amounting to coercion. It was highly, perhaps too, successful. The birth rate has been falling anyway with rising prosperity and better educational and employment opportunities for women. Added to that, the cost of living and lack of suitable family sized accommodation are a deterrent to having children, even if the state were not discouraging it.

The consequence of these factors has been a fall in the fertility rate (the number of births per woman of child bearing age) to a level far below the level needed to maintain a constant population. The Chinese figure is unofficially estimated at 1.2 as against the 2.1 required for replacing the population (by contrast, the US level is 1.8 and India's is 2.4; China's fertility rate appears to be lower even than Japan's). Official projections now show China's population as falling by 2030. Unofficial estimates are that China's population is already falling.

Not merely is there a dearth of children but life expectancy is rising to developed country levels. It is now 77 years from birth (79 for men; 75 for women), just a little less than the USA (79) or the UK (81). So the population is also ageing fast with a corresponding increase of elderly dependents relying on a declining labour force. The government has shown signs of concern at China's population imbalance. To encourage more births, the government has declared a 'two child' policy. But there is no sign at all that the new policy is producing a change in behaviour amongst young people.

How does a declining and ageing work force affect future growth?

The slowdown from around 10% to 6% annual growth can be explained in part by demographics. But 6% is still formidable by the standards of the developed world. What seems to be happening is that the labour market is tightening, with improved wages and working conditions. There are unofficial reports of workers striking and exerting their growing bargaining power where there are labour shortages. But companies are responding to labour shortage by trying to improve productivity. Automation, especially robotics, is becoming much more common in manufacturing. According to the International Federation of Robotics, China has around 100 robots per 10,000 workers in manufacturing. This is half the US level but China is catching up fast both with the installation of machines and the development of the technology behind automation. In addition, some labour intensive processes are moving offshore to poorer countries like Vietnam, again raising productivity. The idea that China must 'run out of steam' because of demographic trends is premature with all the potential that still exists for raising productivity.

But for China to move up into the highest productivity league with the USA, Germany, Japan and Korea also requires innovative, entrepreneurial, creative businesses of the kind that flourish in successful developed economies. The China sceptics argue that a tightly controlled society cannot produce that kind of business environment. They argue that young Chinese are stifled by the lack of free speech and censorship behind the Great Firewall which creates a protected Chinese Internet, filtering out critical material from abroad. As such, it may be difficult to keep China abreast of the most innovative ideas or, even, to keep the best talent in China. All one can say in

10

response is that there is little sign yet of a dampening of Chinese innovation especially in Internet-based technology.

Debt and Financial Instability

Critics have been warning for a decade that Chinese growth is unsustainable because of very high level of debt which, in turn, stems from imbalances in the economy. The International Institute of Finance has estimated that aggregate debt in China is around 317% of GDP. Of that total, public debt-the government's debt -is 48% of GDP and consumer debt, 54% of GDP. Neither of these is exceptional and public debt in particular is one of the lowest of major economies, about half that of the UK or France. But the remainder, corporate debt, is around 215% of GDP, very close to US and UK levels, and it has been growing much more rapidly.

How did this explosion of- corporate- debt happen? We have to go back to the period before the global financial crisis. China's double-digit growth was powered by extraordinary levels of savings domestically (about 50% of GDP in 2007) and large current account surpluses, based on exports of manufactures. Investment was then 41% of GDP and the surplus of savings was mirrored in the massive current account surpluses (9% of GDP). China exported vast quantities of manufactures-as the 'workshop of the world'- benefitting consumers in the West but impacting negatively on some jobs and wages.

Then, the mother of all investment booms

When the financial crisis and deep recession arrived in the West, the pattern of export-led growth was no longer sustainable and China switched rapidly to rely on domestic demand in the form of investment. An enormous investment boom was unleashed, much of it in infrastructure and real estate. It is said that more cement was poured in four years in China than in the previous century in the USA. The boom achieved its immediate objective: double digit Chinese growth was continued, providing jobs and rising living standards at home; the current account surplus disappeared; and China helped to pull the rest of the world out of recession by stimulating a global commodity and capital goods boom.

But the investment was financed largely through the creation of a great deal of dodgy debt. State controlled or owned companies carried out much of the investment, borrowing from banks, also state owned, which concentrated on lending volumes over due diligence. A lot of investment was also driven by eager local officials determined to meet ambitious growth targets set by central government. Local government bodies created financing vehicles to invest themselves or to lend to local enterprises and property developers, often with connections, sometimes corrupt, to officials and party bosses. There were plenty of newly rich investors anxious to buy high yielding assets.

Banks also shifted a lot of their lending 'off balance sheet' into 'shadow banking' to avoid too much regulatory scrutiny; for example selling 'securitised' loans to insurance companies or asset managers. Overall credit growth got up to around 25 or 30% pa. A lot of this credit was of poor quality. Some went to projects which were unlikely to generate a return to service the debt. Much was based on the assumption of a continued bubble in property prices -which would burst. A common assumption was that maybe 20% of lending was bad and would have to be written off.

Which should have led to a financial crisis

For those who saw the credit binge through Western eyes, the conclusion was obvious. China had all the ingredients of a classic debt crisis. Either China would experience the type of collapse seen in the USA or Europe after 2008 as bad debt brought down banks or other institutions and brought the stability of the system into question. Or else China would experience a Japan-style balance-sheet recession as companies held back future investment, giving priority to cleaning up their

12

balance sheets, writing off bad loans and cutting credit. Either way, China was headed for disaster..

But China is not like the USA or Japan. A lot of creditors and debtors are ultimately state-owned or controlled. Loans can be extended and bad debts written down in an orderly manner, with bankrupt state enterprises gradually phased out or restructured. 'Corporate' debt is ultimately government, sovereign debt and the Chinese state has a very comfortable credit standing. With government debt under 50% of GDP, the state could absorb losses from its banks without bringing its sovereign creditworthiness into question. And, ultimately, the Chinese economy is underpinned by vast savings, almost 50% of GDP, so it has no need of foreign borrowing.

So the debt bomb is de-fused

Despite dire warnings from western commentators, the Chinese authorities have been quietly dealing with the debt problem. When President Xi took over in 2013 he identified financial excess, undisciplined lending and high leverage as issues needing attention and the agenda fitted his wider programme of tightening control and moving away from a chaotic, 'Wild East' type of capitalism tolerated by his predecessors. He strengthened regulators so that banks are more conservatively managed, reining in off-balance sheet lending, writing off bad debt and building reserve buffers.

Corruption investigations were used to purge the venal or lax and warn others. Loss making firms were allowed to fold in an orderly way: legal bankruptcies have risen five times in the last few years. He has overseen an expanded and properly regulated bond market so that corporates can raise debt against a background of transparent market disciplines. Strong and booming, regulated, stock markets are there for investors with an appetite for risk and companies seeking risk capital. So, China has not succumbed to the financial instability predicted by the doomsters.

From Investment to Consumption

The debt issue was a symptom of a deeper problem (or problems). China was investing too much and consuming too little. And the investment was often inefficient and unproductive. President Xi and his Prime Minister, Li, have struggled to deal with these issues while also keeping the economy growing at close to the new target level of 6%.

When the economy has threatened to slow down seriously, as in the wake of Covid lock-down, the quick fix is a burst of credit expansion supporting new investment. Such intervention has kept growth going but added to the problems around poor investment and debt. Instead of just relying on credit expansion the government has also used some of the 'fiscal space', provided by its low official debt, to borrow on its own account and to run a fiscal deficit to sustain growth. But, by the standards of Western economies, and Japan, the post-Covid economic stimulus of around 5% of GDP is very modest. Nor are there good prospects of relying on export growth to pull the economy along, with the world in slump and Trump conducting trade war against China.

The regime has a dilemma. If it pumps more credit into the economy it creates more questionable investment. If it doesn't, it gets into the politically dangerous territory of slow growth, unemployment and curtailed living standards.

Such conditions would strengthen the hands of those who are nervous about reform where it involves difficult decisions: axing loss-making, inefficient, 'zombie' companies, in sectors like steel, aluminium, coal and cement especially in parts of the country like the North East where there are fewer alternative jobs. Yet failure to tackle these issues, and to raise the productivity of investment, acts in turn as a drag on the economy.

So far, under Xi, there has been a determined push to raise the productivity of state-owned firms, bringing in private capital, and demanding higher returns. And, even with Covid, the economy has been kept going. But future success depends on new sources of demand: the Chinese consumer.

So, how does China become a consumer economy?

The potential is vast. On a purchasing power basis, the average Chinese is still substantially poorer than the average Korean, let alone the average Japanese or American. Using IMF data, China's GDP per head – a rough proxy for living standards – is just over $20,000: a bit less than Thailand or Mexico; under half the UK level of $48,000 or Korea's $45,000: and less than a third of the USA, at $67,000 (or Hong Kong which is at the same level). There is a lot of scope for 'catch-up' in terms of living standards.

To take the case of the car industry, it is unlikely, given space constraints and population densities, that China will ever approach US levels of car ownership. Despite that, China already has a bigger, overall car market than the USA with sales of over 20 million vehicles a year. In 2017, 24.7 million cars were sold in China as against 17.1 million in the USA. China then had two bad years (down to 21.4 million sales in 2019) but demand has surged again following the end of the Covid 19 lockdown: sales were up 11% in June 2020 over the same month in 2019.

And there is plenty of evidence from the big cities that a 'new economy' is emerging with rapid growth of demand for entertainment, healthcare and retail. To take an example, cinema screens saw an expansion of over 35% per annum after 2010 to 70,000 screens in 2019, the world's largest market by some way (albeit that there is now a lot of spare capacity).

The Chinese consumer driving the new economy is to be found on-line rather than with a shopping bag. China is already by far the largest e-commerce market in the world and it is growing at around 10% pa. (there was a 16% growth from June 2019 to June 2020, post Covid). On-line shopping accounted for 3% of retail sales in 2010 and the figure is now around 17%. Looking at comparative data, the Chinese market is around $1.9 trillion as against just under $600 billion in the USA with 80% of payment by mobile apps as against 30% in the USA. Ali Baba, the leading e-commerce platform, has more business than Amazon and eBay combined.

With so much of the economy, not just retail, based on the Internet, China still has a great deal of untapped potential. Despite having the largest number of Internet users by some way, Chinese penetration is still only 55% of individuals as against 95% in the UK, 87% in the USA and 35% in India. What all this tells us is that there is a vast, rapidly growing but still only partially developed, market for Internet based activity which gives continued scope for growing consumption as well as a source of demand, and innovation, for Chinese firms.

Producing a new economy

A new, consumer-based and service-based economy is replacing the old industrial economy of steel and cement.

When the reform process started in the late 1970's, industry accounted for almost 50% of the economy, agriculture 30% and services 20%. The most recent estimates have that balance shifting to 38% for industry (including construction), 8 % for agriculture and 54% for services. The industrial sector is still disproportionately large. But a survey carried out in 2016 showed that in Beijing and Shanghai over 70% of the city economy was contributed by the service sector and other big cities showed the emergence of this 'new economy' based on personal consumption and services.

Much of this consumption is led by the middle class which in China is defined as household incomes of $24,000 a year, which is around 30% of the population. It is not just the emerging urban middle class which is spending more. One of the government's key priorities is to mop up the remaining pockets of extreme poverty. There were 30 million people living on $1 a day in 2017, many of them in remote communities on China's periphery. China's great historic achievement has been the lifting of 850 million people out of extreme poverty since reforms began. Completing the project of poverty alleviation (at least in this minimal way) is likely to be completed this year or next. And broadening the base of consumers adds to demand.

There are other trends, too, working towards a consumer-driven economy. Consumer debt is very low by international standards: 40% of GDP, roughly half of US levels and well under half of UK levels (currently close to 90%). And even though the number, as well as the proportion, of young people is shrinking thanks to low fertility rates, the under 35's have a significantly higher propensity to consume: an estimated 15% annual growth in spending, twice that of older citizens. Chinese young people, especially, have developed a taste for foreign travel and brands. Unlike the former Soviet Union, China has not tried to imprison its population. An estimated 100 million go abroad every year, to study, shop or for sight-seeing. And inside China there has been rapidly growing demand for the products of leading global brands like Pepsi, McDonalds, Starbucks and Disney.

The Chinese are becoming the world's leading consumers.

Political Leadership and Economic Reform

China is making the switch from heavy industry to consumer-based services. But this change will not just happen through serendipity. Much now depends on the political leadership pressing ahead with necessary economic reform while coping with domestic resistance to painful change and the increasingly threatening external environment: the new Cold War.

It is difficult to get one's head around the fact that currently the most successful capitalist economy in the world, in terms of growth, investment and innovation is run by the Chinese Communist Party which takes Marx, Lenin and Mao as its ideological inspiration. In fact, the Communist Party is no longer, remotely, a revolutionary party. It is the Chinese ruling class: an organisation of over 80 million members which provides continuity, cohesion and discipline within what is in effect a new dynasty. Its legitimacy - its 'mandate from heaven' – derives not from elections or from revolutionary heroics but from a form of social contract: the public accept its rule in return for its ability to provide stability and, within that, competent economic management permitting rising living standards and near-full employment.

Much of the Western commentary is about a newly assertive China, under a bullying, dictatorial, leader seeking to throw its weight about internationally. Things look different from inside China. The priority is the economy and the conservative maxim prevails that China must prioritise its internal affairs. That means consolidating the party's political grip on the country while at the same time being pragmatic and flexible on economic policy. That was the formula of Deng Tsao Ping, the architect of modern China; not the dogma and revolutionary chaos of Chairman Mao. President Xi pays homage to Mao but is following the Deng playbook.

Which means updating 'state capitalism'

What has changed in the 7 years of President Xi's leadership is a more personalised and centralised style of decision-making with the associated advantages and disadvantages.

There was a fierce crackdown on corruption which involved some genuine corruption and some vengeful attacks on opponents and critics. Concentration of power in Xi's hands and the expectation that he will continue in power, rather than pass on the leadership like his immediate predecessors, has created a more authoritarian atmosphere.

The inevitable consequence is more obsequiousness and a reluctance by subordinates to make difficult decisions, to make even constructive criticisms or to pass bad news up the chain (as with the Wuhan pandemic). But Xi is clearly not a fool or a megalomaniac and all his pronouncements and actions suggest that he understands the value of pragmatic competence.

This pragmatic competence has several elements which define Xi's model of 'state capitalism'.

The first is the introduction of more market disciplines and private sector management systems into the public sector as a way of making it more commercial and accelerating the shift from the inefficient industries of old. The second is to nurture private enterprise but within a framework of state (and Party) direction. The expression of state direction is in the form of an active industrial policy, mobilising the research and business community behind new, hopefully world-beating technologies with policies which resemble those successfully used in Japan and Korea.

The effectiveness of 'state capitalism' depends on the politics: in particular, Xi's leadership as head of an authoritarian one party state. Western democracy is explicitly rejected. And the recent descent into the populism of Trump and Brexit has reduced whatever appeal it may have had to members of the educated elite.

40 years ago Deng made a clear distinction between economic liberalisation, which he launched to great effect, and political liberalisation which he abhorred, predicting, correctly, the disintegration of the Soviet Union under Gorbachev.

The man who presided over the greatest achievement in poverty reduction in history was also the author of the Tiananmen Square massacre.

Xi is his descendant and shares his priorities. His particular refinement is to develop techniques of surveillance of the population which also make use of and help develop frontier data technologies like AI – *artificial intelligence*.

Will Xi survive? Very likely. Will he succeed? Probably.

Chapter 3.

Is China's Economic Success Good for the Rest of Us?

The emergence, in little more than a generation, of a new economic superpower and the lifting of hundreds of millions from poverty to middle income should be good news. It has often seemed so. Western business has generally treated the creation of a vast new market for consumer products, capital goods and services as an opportunity. Western consumers have enjoyed lower import prices directly or through Chinese participation in supply chains. Commodity exporters have enjoyed the benefits of the rapidly growing Chinese market for foodstuffs and industrial raw materials. Chinese investment has provided, in the last decade, a source of growth in an otherwise weak, global, economy. For those who believe in the benefits of an open trading system and economic integration, China's economic success has been a boon.

But it would be naïve to believe that everyone is a winner. Some are losers and losers matter. And they certainly matter when they are more influential than the winners.

At the centre of the new Cold War is the USA for whom China represents serious competition and loss of a dominance enjoyed for three quarters of a century. If geo-economics is a zero-sum game, 'America first' to 'America second' is a loss in a game of two. The geo-economics is reinforced by the resurfacing of the view that international trade is also a zero-sum game: the idea that 'winners', who have surpluses, are offset by 'losers' who have deficits.

Trump's obsession with bilateral deficits in trade with China reflects this 'mercantilist' approach which last prevailed two centuries ago. And, within countries, there are winners and losers too: losers being groups of workers in competing industries in the importing country who have lost incomes and jobs. President Trump has skilfully managed to build a strong political platform in the US around the idea that China is a winner (or was becoming one under his predecessors), and the US a loser, based on three elements: the geo-economics, the mercantilist view of trade and the disadvantaged workers.

So, what are the facts?

Trade winners and losers

As of 2019, China was the world's biggest exporter of goods by some way: $2.5 trillion as against $1.6 tn. for the USA and $1.5 tn. for Germany (out of total world trade of $18.7 tn.). The USA imports more: $2.6 tn. as against $2.1 tn. for China and $1.2 tn. for Germany. Overall China conducts more trade but enjoys a trade surplus, albeit of the same order of magnitude as Germany, while the USA has a substantial deficit.

The position is changed somewhat when we consider trade in services where the USA has a large surplus and China a deficit. US services exports were estimated at $0.83 tn. in 2019 and imports $0.58 tn.; China $0.23 tn. and $0.53 tn.; Germany $0.35 tn. and $0.37 tn.

These figures have to be treated with care and are often the subject of political mischief. Aggregate export and import figures for goods are subject to a great deal of distortion and double counting because of integrated supply chains. Chinese 'exports' of iPhones, for example, will incorporate US-made chips and other components from a variety of countries, particularly Japan, Korea and Taiwan. The valuation of components as they cross borders will also have more to do with corporate tax policy than their cost. It is estimated that

Chinese exports and imports are probably overstated by a factor of 30% and US imports and exports by 20%.

The figures, additionally, include a lot of Chinese 'exports' to and 'imports' from Hong Kong which is like adding trade in and out of California to US data.

Services statistics are even shakier. Tourism, for example, for which China has a large deficit, includes a lot of hidden capital flows. A Chinese family visiting London or San Francisco may well be involved in spending money buying a flat as well as looking at the sights. Capital flight is a major issue for China as the nouveaux riches seek to hedge against political risk or to build up an international portfolio, especially as the Chinese currency is undervalued in terms of purchasing power. Yet the true figures are largely hidden.

The nonsensical economics of bilateral deficits

For these reasons, to treat trade figures as some sort of measure of national 'success' and to treat imbalances, especially bilateral imbalances, as a measure of 'fairness' is wrong. Yet US-China economic diplomacy is built around it.

There is also a deeper reason why this way of calculating economic performance, looking at trade in isolation, isn't meaningful. The international movement of capital leads to trade imbalances, of goods and services, simply being a reflection of imbalances between domestic savings (and consumption) and investment.

If a country saves more than it can productively invest, the surplus savings have to go somewhere and, in practice, flow overseas. There is also a glut of production over what can be consumed and this is exported as a trade surplus (mathematically, the trade surplus should match the export of capital). In the case of China, it used to have vast savings surpluses with a counterpart in large trade surpluses amounting to as much as 10% of production. These trade surpluses, manifested mainly in exports of manufactured goods, were the basis of China's early growth after Deng's reforms. They had a counterpart in the export of capital which took the form of purchases of US dollar assets, forming China's foreign exchange reserves.

The big investment boom of the last decade has narrowed the imbalance between savings and investment in China. The current emphasis on boosting consumption as a source of growth is, at last, dealing with the issue and China in 2020 is estimated to have just about eliminated the imbalances. The estimated current account surplus is under 1% of GDP as against the 9 to 10% of GDP a decade ago. Indeed China is no longer one of the 'surplus' countries in contrast to Germany (6% of GDP estimated for 2020), Japan (2.5%), Switzerland, Taiwan and Singapore (all 10% or more).

These 'surplus' economies are the mirror image of 'deficit' countries where the imbalance between savings and investment is in the opposite direction: a deficit of saving and excessive consumption leading to the import of savings and current account deficits. However the major current account deficits have shrunk in recent years and are, in total, now under 2% of GDP for the USA.

The major deficit economies no longer have a grievance that China is artificially creating trade surpluses at their expense, to the extent that such grievances were ever meaningful. In any event, Trump's complaint is more specific: that China should be exporting less to the USA or importing more from the USA; even if that means exporting more to Japan and Germany and Switzerland and importing less from them. But, then, the real quarrel is with the present-day 'surplus' economies, Japan for example, not China.

Currency as an Economic weapon

One of the allegations made against China, by Trump and others, is that the exchange rate has been manipulated to promote exports contributing to its trade and current account surpluses. In the 1990's and 2000's there was some basis for the complaint that China was a 'currency manipulator'. In 1994 there was a big devaluation and the yuan was pegged to the dollar at 8.3 yuan (or renminbi) to the dollar for over a decade. The effect was to make exports highly competitive in price and also to discourage domestic consumption (and create an excess of savings).

China acquired large current account surpluses (around 6% of GDP). After 2005 however there was a gradual appreciation of the currency reinforced by relatively high inflation in China which meant that in real terms the value of the currency relative to the dollar increased by around 60%. There was a rebalancing of the economy with greatly reduced savings surpluses and current account surpluses. The idea that China was artificially depressing its currency to boost its trade ceased to have any substance.

But in 2015 there was a massive outflow of capital leading to an involuntary devaluation. Chinese savers had been limited by capital controls on what they could send overseas. The dam burst with large scale, technically illegal, transfers of funds. The government recognised reality and partially liberalised the capital account (though some controls remain in place). Since then China has been attached to a basket of 24 currencies and the authorities have sought to maintain stability in real terms (the real effective exchange rate).

They have been broadly successful in doing so. What this means in practical terms is that China does not, and cannot, use its currency as a weapon in trade competition. One requirement to keep the exchange rate stable is to inhibit capital flight which, these days, depends more on its interest rate and monetary policies, and overall economic confidence, than porous capital controls.

In the last few months, worry has grown in China that the USA's dispute with China will escalate way beyond trade balances and exchange rates. What if the US started to treat China as a rogue state like Iran and North Korea and tried to stop China trading altogether?

The USA could disrupt the payments system which Chinese firms use. In technical terms, this means blocking access to CHIPS, a US based clearing system for dollar transactions and/or SWIFT, based in Europe, which facilitates payments. China is in an altogether different league from Iran and has a massive amount of trade with the USA. But the mere fact that these ideas are being canvassed, even if only on the fringes, is likely to make China do some rethinking on international finance.

One idea which will gain some traction is speeding up the process of trying to make the yuan/renminbi a global currency so that China can transact business without recourse to the dollar. That in turn makes full convertability more attractive though the economic disciplines required to make it work are very demanding. It is possible however that the dispute could accelerate Chinese long-term ambitions to have a global currency, competing with and eventually displacing the dollar.

From Free Trade to Trade War

The post-war trading system is built on the notion that an open trading system is of great positive economic value, overall. Both developed and developing countries have prospered on the back of it, latterly including China. But protectionist arguments have had a strong minority following until President Trump adopted them. To be fair to Trump, friction over trade imbalances goes back as much as 30 years when Japan, rather than China, was still the bogey-man: with large current account surpluses stemming from an excess of savings.

Tariffs were imposed on Japanese cars but had little effect except to raise prices to consumers .The Japanese financial crisis however burst the Japanese economic bubble, effectively stopping growth, and gradually anxiety shifted to China.

China, as part of its reform programme, had joined the World Trade Organisation (in 2001) and accepted the disciplines associated with it, though as a developing economy China enjoyed 'special and differential' treatment and was not required to reciprocate the market opening which its exporters enjoyed. Crucially, China enjoyed Most Favoured Nation (MFN) treatment so that the tariff barriers its exporters faced were the same as those facing other exporting countries. It could no longer be discriminated against (in fact, the USA had already agreed to MFN status some years earlier).

The rapid growth and scale of China's manufactured exports had major benefits to consumers in the West and could be said to have contributed to lower inflation in goods overall. The prices of clothing and footwear, appliances, household furnishings, toys and tools have fallen over time. But in the USA there has been a growing trend to blame China for the stagnation of real wages and living standards and the de-industrialisation of 'rust belt' states. An influential study by Autor, Dorn and Hanson has shown that, if the impact of China is isolated, maybe a quarter of job losses could be attributed to the China 'shock'. But these findings relate to two decades ago; and it is quite possible that many of the jobs would have gone anyway due to productivity-raising technology. Nonetheless such analysis fed the negativity of politicians.

And the political negativity is growing

This negativity surfaced in the early 1990's when President Clinton had to persuade Congress to renew MFN provisions for China. Since then, there has been growing hostility to Chinese imports in the US labour movement and amongst Democrat lawmakers.

Businesses have been divided. Some companies have benefitted hugely from trade with China. Boeing has sold around 2000 planes and made huge profits from China's expansion in aviation. General Motors managed to turn around its business from bankruptcy on the back of car sales in China; Ford has also done extremely well there. Iconic American brands like Starbucks, KFC, Proctor and Gamble and Kraft have also had great success usually through their Chinese subsidiaries rather than cross-border trade. Apple has built its highly profitable global business making appliances like iPhones around complex international supply chains with a major Chinese production element. But there has also been a loud volume of complaint from other businesses about Chinese trade and investment barriers, weak intellectual property rights and the sense that there isn't a 'level playing field'.

President Trump has been able to gain political traction by bringing together the discontents of workers and businesses.

His initial foray into trade protectionism and tariffs, however, had little to do with China. It was to renegotiate the NAFTA agreement with Mexico and Canada; to take the USA out of the Trans-Pacific Partnership (which excluded China); and to impose tariffs on imported steel and aluminium from various sources to give protection to industries whose voters had supported him. The motivation was to demonstrate his skill in negotiation – *The Art of the Deal* – and to 'win' concessions through trade warfare: Making America Great Again.

China came to the fore in part because there was already substantial, cross-party, lobbying against China, reinforced by security concerns. A crucial influence was a key adviser, Peter Navarro, a former Harvard academic, whose background gave Trump's prejudices some intellectual respectability and whose book and film, *Death by China*, had focussed the attention of the group of economic nationalists around Trump on the 'threat' of China.

Navarro also linked the China trade issue with the President's obsession with bilateral deficits. As discussed above, the focus on bilateral deficits is seriously misleading. But the metric has one considerable advantage: it enables Trump to quantify his 'wins' (and, for that matter, for the Chinese to demonstrate their 'concessions'). The initial objective of Trump's war was limited and narrowly focussed.

Trade war breaks out

The opening salvo in the trade war with China was fired in May 2018. The Trump administration opened negotiations demanding that the bilateral trade deficit (then around $375bn. for goods) be cut by $200bn. over two years; that China should abandon a wide variety of subsidies, tariffs and interventions; should accept restrictions on Chinese investment in the USA in technology sectors; and should not retaliate. To demonstrate seriousness, 10% tariffs were imposed on $200 bn. of Chinese goods. The humiliating tone seemed calculated to cause offense but the Chinese response was muted. They assumed that Trump's aggression was 'sound and fury' signifying not very much.

There were some retaliatory measures but a bilateral negotiating process was initiated outside the WTO. There have been further rounds of US tariffs imposed at a higher rate (25%) and covering more products and further retaliation directed at items politically sensitive in the USA, like soya beans. The Chinese have, however, shown a willingness to negotiate, seemingly making the calculation that Trump simply wants a symbolic victory to parade at the November Presidential elections and that any concessions need only be cosmetic.

That calculation may however be wrong.

Relations with China have deteriorated rapidly with the rows over responsibility for the Covid pandemic and over Hong Kong. The US administration has widened the dispute to exclude Chinese technology companies, notably Huawei, from the USA and a process of decoupling is gaining momentum.

There are two big conclusions to draw about the wider implications of the trade war. First, the USA is out on its own. The EU and other Chinese trade partners have plenty of gripes about Chinese trade practices but are pursuing them through the World Trade Organisation or bilaterally. They also have their own trade disputes with the USA which, in some cases, are more serious and threatening than those with China.

Second, the usual business voices speaking up for freer trade in the USA have been silent or ineffectual in the arguments about a trade war with China. That raises the question of China's treatment of foreign investors and the seemingly ambivalent attitude to China of companies operating there.

China and Foreign Investors

There is a big gap between the rhetoric employed in the 'trade war,' in which China is accused of excluding foreign companies or discriminating against them, and the survey data on foreign investment which suggests that China is actually a relatively attractive destination (compared to other leading emerging markets) and friendly to business, foreign as well as Chinese.

The World Bank publishes an annual survey on the 'ease of doing business' (www.doingbusiness.org) which relates to business in general rather than foreign owned companies in particular. The metrics are rankings based on a variety of indicators: ease of starting a business; availability of construction permits; electricity supply; registration of property; access to credit; corporate governance including protection of minority investors.

Overall, China ranks far ahead of most developing countries and compares well with many developed economies. China's overall ranking is 31, a little lower than Japan (29) and Germany (22) but ahead of France (32), Netherlands (42) and Italy (58). China is a long way behind the leading western countries (USA, 6th and UK 8th) or the more business friendly

Asian countries: Singapore, Korea, Taiwan (respectively, 2, 5 and 15 in the rankings) but way ahead of India (63rd), Vietnam (70) and Pakistan (108). Significantly, Hong Kong, whose future is now in doubt, ranks 3rd.

The overall direction of travel, reflecting Xi's reforms, is to liberalise. The World Bank, in its report on 2019 listed China in the top 10 for improvements, especially in simplifying bureaucratic processes, legal protections and smoothness of insolvency proceedings. But there remain significant weaknesses: bureaucracy, corruption and intellectual property protection (though the last of these appears to be improving.)

For many foreign investors, the relevant comparison is not with the USA or the UK but with the other big emerging market economies: India, Brazil and Mexico. Forbes has recently made such a comparison which shows China more attractive in key respects: tax (a 25% corporation tax rate as against 35% in India and Brazil); logistics such as ports, airports, railways and roads, where China is way ahead; corruption, bad, around Indian levels, but not as bad as Brazil or Mexico or Vietnam; low crime; and quality and cost of labour though wage costs are rising rapidly.

What appears to be happening is that, under Xi, the private sector is more controlled, to avoid excess and 'Wild East' behaviour and to encourage adherence to party 'guidance'; but that there are also clearer and more transparent rules with more of a 'rule of law,' at least applying to commercial matters.

There is a list of grumbles

But there are specific issues which have led to the complaint that China is not as welcoming to foreign business as a confident, successful, capitalist country should be or as welcoming as (most) Western countries are to Chinese companies.

The first, a crucial area for foreign investors with advanced technology or valuable brands and copyright, and a source of major grievance in the past, is the theft of intellectual property rights, sometimes by partner companies and sometimes by pirates who go unpunished. It is clear however that under President Xi there has been a big drive to improve protection of IP and to channel disputes into IP courts where they can be dealt with by due process outside of political interference. Referrals have doubled in the last few years and it is said that 90% of cases brought by foreigners are being won. The pirates who lose cases are now tracked and penalised by credit black-listing so cannot continue unhindered as before.

A second complaint is the requirement in many sectors that investors form joint ventures with local partners or transfer valuable technology. These obligations are now being relaxed. In any event, no one at all familiar with emerging markets will find these demands surprising. It has been a basic responsibility of economic ministers in all developing economies that have some bargaining power to ensure that investors don't just make money in their country but contribute to development.

China has more bargaining power and skill than most but is doing nothing which isn't common practice in Brazil or Saudi Arabia let alone India. It could reasonably be argued that whilst China is no longer a developing economy there are also developed countries which make demands on their investors: for example Japan, Korea and France. Even such an open, welcoming, host country as the UK tries to impose conditions on some foreign takeovers.

I know and I have done it.

Third, and most compelling, there are sectors effectively barred to major investors for what the Chinese would regard as security reasons but others would call, simply, censorship. The most important are the big US data and social media companies: Facebook, Google, Twitter, WhatsApp, Instagram, U-tube.

This discrimination can operate in two ways. One is simply by exclusion from certain activities. The other is by censorship of the Internet which China does by establishing gateways where incoming data can be sifted and sorted by state agencies policing the Great Firewall. By doing this, the Chinese are putting themselves on weak ground to counter, for example, the attacks on Huawei. And they have turned into adversaries some of the most influential businessmen in the USA.

But the position is actually more nuanced. Most of these companies are doing business in China (in addition to Apple which has major Chinese operations). Nor is censorship an issue in itself; after all, many of us are clamouring for Facebook to be more assiduous in filtering out hate material, child porn, fake news and terrorist propaganda.

A story of successes and failures

A lot of foreign companies have failed in China, contributing to the idea that China is a hostile environment for foreigners and these experiences have fed the current Cold War narrative. But critical analysis by Western management schools suggests that the main reasons for failure are business related: underestimating the strength of Chinese competition and poor dealings with local company partners and a tendency to impose a global or US business model and to play down the value of deep local knowledge and understanding.

China is, after all, one of the biggest recipients of inward foreign direct investment especially among emerging markets. There has been a mixed experience but enough investor successes to reinforce the idea that business rather than politics is what matters. Car manufacturers - BMW, JLR, GM and Ford, and their Chinese joint venture partners – and fast-moving consumer goods have produced major success stories: the latter group including beer, coffee shops, fast food, films.

Starbucks has 3,400 shops. KFC has 30% of its market, having adapted its chicken to regional tastes. Kraft foods, McDonalds, Proctor & Gamble and makers of sportswear shoes have all, apparently, been successful in revenue and profitability terms (Nike claims to be getting double digit growth every quarter over five years). The Swedish IKEA is extremely popular and has adapted to the Chinese dislike for DIY by delivering its kits and assembling them.

There are moreover many successes that are not confined to consumer goods. Shell's massive Nanhai petrochemical complex is now undergoing its third big expansion and is producing good returns for Shell after decades of joint venture working with a local partner. Even in the highly politicised and exposed area of high tech, America's leading micro-chip maker, Qualcomm, claims to generate two thirds of its revenue in China and is a major client of Huawei in China. And super-giant Apple is believed to generate 15% of its global revenue from China including Hong Kong (and Taiwan).

The failures include the tech companies, with the important exception of Apple, and perhaps Microsoft (with LinkedIn).

Government obstruction may have played a part but the strength of local competition did also. Amazon had a strong local competitor, Alibaba, now a global company; E-bay was pushed out by Taobao (which realised that Chinese customers would not part with goods until they had cash in hand); AirBnB lost out to Tuija; Uber spent $2bn and had a strong local partner, Baidu, but could not compete with Didi; Google struggled to compete with Baidu even before its search engine was subject to censorship, but hasn't given up and is trying to develop an AI centre and local mobile apps. There are, even here, some success stories. LinkedIn has over 30 million users and seems to have established a strong, secure, presence.

Crucially, China is now opening its markets to foreign investors in the finance sector (at precisely the time when the USA is trying to close them). Foreign ownership limits have been lifted on securities firms, life insurers and asset managers. Payments systems like Mastercard are now welcome- in theory.

The conclusion has to be that while many foreign companies have flourished in China and some have failed, the problem for the latter has been as much the heat of the competition as the cold of government control. We would normally regard competition as a good thing in markets. So who are the Chinese competitors?

The Chinese Multinational

The best description of the Chinese economic model is that it is 'state capitalist': an amalgam of private and public enterprise, competitive markets and central control. In terms of the enterprises which make up 'state capitalism' they are essentially of two kinds (in practice there are several more, like local municipal enterprises and other small and medium sized companies).

The first are the increasingly commercial and competitive state enterprises (SOEs). Many are now publicly quoted as well as state owned like Sinopec and Petro-China, energy companies in the style of Saudi Aramco or Norway's Statoil; China Mobile; or SAIC motors. There has been a move to set tighter financial criteria for state enterprises, bringing them closer to the private sector by mimicking enhancement of shareholder value. There is also a process of developing mixed ownership including listings on stock exchanges to attract private investment.

Then, there are those companies that are genuinely private and in some cases have been established by charismatic, internationally admired, entrepreneurs like Jack Ma, founder of Alibaba (China's Amazon), and also the digital payments company Ant, currently making one of the world's largest IPOs; Ren Zhengfei of Huawei; 'Pony Ma' of Tencent (owner of WeChat); Zhang Yimin of Byte Dance (the owner of Tik Tok); Wang Chuanfu of BYD the electric car maker; Eric Yuan of Zoom, Robin Li and Eric Yu of Baidu, the leading AI company; Li Shufu of Geely (the owner of Saab); Xu Jiayin of Evergrande, the real estate and development giant; and the pioneering Rong Yiren of China International Trust, CITIC.

These enterprises vary greatly in their closeness to the Chinese government, the extent of their overseas exposure and their approach to corporate organisation. In many ways they resemble big Western companies which have evolved rapidly from private to public companies but retain the personality (and control) of their founders, having not yet become impersonal corporates: like Mark Zuckerberg of Facebook or Jeff Bezos of Amazon.

And there is not just a layer of established Chinese multinationals but a deep pool of start-ups which gain scale in China's vast and growing market and then branch out overseas. The climate in China is generally benign for business leaders who keep out of politics and there is no obvious retreat from the entrepreneurial environment introduced to China by Deng Xiaoping with his fabled comment: 'to get rich is glorious'.

China is now producing dozens of companies with international standards of management performance and corporate governance. Many of these raise large amounts of capital overseas. Chinese companies have raised over $250 bn in US capital markets since 2014, $ 415 bn since the turn of the century. Chinese companies listed in the USA have a market capitalisation of over a trillion dollars.

These companies do however now face a degree of uncertainty over their future after the banning, effectively, of Huawei from the USA (as well as Australia and the UK) and attempts to undermine, perhaps destroy, the company by cutting off US-made components; added to which has been the threat to close TikTok in the US.

There are threats from the White House, so far not acted upon, to make it more difficult for Chinese companies to list in the

US. Such a move, if made, could be counter-productive, weakening the incentive to adopt Western standards of governance and audit and strengthening Chinese capital markets.

And Chinese capital markets, especially the stock exchanges, are now more carefully regulated and shareholder friendly than before, and provide a major, growing, source of new equity as well as share trading in 4000 listed companies for Chinese as well as overseas investors. Shenzhen is currently the world's best performing major stock exchange. Hong Kong is enjoying a boom in IPOs, despite the politics.

The boom in Chinese stocks has added $2 trillion to the value of China's top ten non-state companies since president Xi come to power. US funds have invested roughly $200 bn. in the last year alone in China, and Blackrock and JP Morgan are shifting fund management operations there. There is an obvious incentive for fund managers to shift their investment portfolios to China when China accounts for around 15% of the world economy but only 5% of world equity markets. In addition, Chinese stocks are not generally perceived to be inflated. However, one of the biggest threats posed by the new 'Cold War' is the suggestion, so far not acted upon, to force US investors to sell their stocks in China.

The complaint of some Western competitors and governments is that this vast reservoir of entrepreneurial talent and business competition is, nonetheless, beholden to the Chinese state. Evidence for this assertion is the fact that some companies publish obsequious statements of political support for President and Party (not that that is unknown outside China); there are party committees embedded in companies (the Chinese would claim that this is not unlike German co-determination); and that companies have a legal obligation to support Chinese national security (as do Western companies faced, for example, with sanctions regimes).

There are, as with leading companies in the USA, Europe and Japan, often connections to government and, where there are genuine national security concerns, it is right to be careful. But the vast majority of Chinese firms are commercial, not political, in their motivation. The key issue for the future, in technology sectors, is where the balance lies.

Chapter 4.

Technology Wars: the New Battleground

There are several ingredients in the new Cold War, with China: trade, military security, human rights and political differences plus the issues which have emerged in 2020 like the handling of the pandemic and Hong Kong. But I would argue that the key factor, transcending the others, is technology: the fear of the United States, in particular, that it is being overtaken by China in key, new, developments like 5G, big data and AI and that this, in turn, will adversely affect the economic, military and geo-political balance in the long run.

But how far is Chinese technology ahead or behind the USA (and other competitors, as in the EU). Is China a leader or a follower?

Who Is Winning The Technology Race?

The usual assumption is that the USA is ahead of the world in most key technologies and China is seeking to catch up, copying or – allegedly – stealing the ideas. However the story is much more complex and rapidly moving.

Dennis Wang has produced one of the most thorough recent analyses of technology trends and he identifies several areas where China is clearly leading the world. One is high-speed rail. With such trains already running and others under construction there should be around 45,000 kilometres of track by 2030, far more than in any other country.

Another is e-commerce. China now has the largest number of users – 200 million a day – shopping on line. And this level of use has grown from virtually nothing 5 or 6 years ago.

Linked to e-commerce is the development of mobile payments. China is already close to becoming the first cash-less society thanks to systems developed by WeChatPay (based on We Chat's 900 million social media users) and Alipay (an app of Jack Ma's Alibaba on-line retailer which has evolved into the giant Ant Group).

Then, there are drones. The Chinese company DJI produces the largest number of drones and applications of its drone technology for commercial purposes. And last there is the provision of instant on-line services: not just taxis and deliveries but cleaning, plumbing, child-care and medical diagnosis.

All these examples are practical applications of new technology. More important are the core technologies on which these are based. There are three big, overlapping, technologies: telecommunications; AI or Artificial Intelligence; Big Data. Of these, China could claim to be ahead in 5G because of Huawei which has had more 5G patents filed than any other company and twice as many as the nearest US competitor, Qualcomm.

But there are some fields in which China has struggled. One is semi-conductors. Only around 16% of semi-conductors used in China are made in China and of those only half are made in Chinese companies. The telecommunications company ZTE was crippled, and almost bankrupted, in 2018 when the US imposed a ban on sales of components to the company after ZTE had breached American sanctions on Iran.

Major efforts are being made to develop state-of-the-art Chinese semi-conductors in the Wuhan-based SMIC and a Huawei subsidiary, HiSilicon, while the world's leading semi-conductor company, Taiwanese TSCM, is expanding manufacturing on the mainland.

China's Underlying Technological Strengths

The semi-conductor experience raises the bigger question as to how equipped China is to catch up and then lead in these key technologies. A lazy assumption in the West is that Chinese companies are good at copying and stealing but lack creativity and innovation. There are however several grounds for believing that China has the capacity to emerge as the winner in any competition for technological leadership.

First, scale matters. China's vast home market provides for economies of scale as well as a test-bed for trying out new technologies, even if there are barriers overseas. The ability to generate strong, sustained, growth based on consumption enables firms to innovate and compete in an expanding market.

Second, China's very high rate of savings provides a large pool of capital. There are many high-net-worth individuals looking for big returns. Angel investor networks flourish. The appetite for high risk, high return investment has engendered a big venture capital market, now bigger than in the USA ($31 billion in 2018)

Third there is an enormous reservoir of highly skilled, scientifically trained, manpower. China has tripled its number of universities over a decade to over 3000, hosting over 40 million students. Not all are of the same quality but the focus on STEM (science, technology, engineering and maths) will ensure that China soon has the world's largest pool of STEM graduates. And the encouragement to Chinese students to study abroad (very different from the former USSR) establishes a benchmark of standards as well as foreign language, mainly English, proficiency. At the top end of skills, the Thousand Talents programme is establishing a cadre of very advanced students, for fields such as AI, with a minimum of an overseas PhD and evidence of entrepreneurial flair.

Fourth, the frontier technologies linked to AI will require vast quantities of data as their raw material. In China, data is available in abundance helped by lack of privacy laws and few constraints on its use. The main e-commerce platforms, with hundreds of millions of users, are a rich source. Some of the data sources would not be tolerated in Western societies including 200 million cameras, which, an addition to their uncontroversial uses in traffic management and crime prevention, form the backbone of a system of surveillance.

Fifth, the government is immensely supportive of science and innovation and has deep pockets to back up its interventions. The state, as in the West, can be wasteful and misdirect resources but it can also take a longer view than corporate shareholders. The current planning framework, Made in China: 2025, is designed to build up 'self-reliance' in Chinese semiconductors and sophisticated microchips and to give maximum support to the frontier technologies like AI. Western critics of this kind of active industry policy attack it from two contradictory directions: that it won't work or that it will work and represents unfair competition.

Finally, and crucially, big government is allied to a highly entrepreneurial culture fostered by government. There are tax breaks for investors who support start-ups and innovation parks to provide facilities for new companies and to act as incubators. The Communist Party has no problem with the slogan of an 'innovation state' and President Xi's institutional reforms, described earlier, are designed to create more orderly, rules-based, markets for those entrepreneurs who keep out of political trouble. Time will tell if this kind of hybrid system will work. In the meantime the Western world, especially the USA, is unsure whether to try to beat it, join it or crush it. At present, crushing is in fashion. As with Huawei.

5G and Huawei

One area where Chinese technology had appeared to be overtaking that of the West is 5G. Huawei is the world's largest integrated telecommunications company with base stations in

180 countries. It has a turnover of $125 billion and almost 200,000 employees. It operates at a scale significantly higher than its competitors in telecommunications equipment, like Nokia and Erikson in Europe, and is well ahead of Qualcomm in the USA. This year, it has also overtaken Samsung to be the largest smart-phone provider. It led the world with 4G technology and its formidable R and D capacity, with a $15bn research budget, is believed to have put it well ahead in patenting and introducing 5G.

5G matters since it makes improvements in several dimensions: computational speeds, potentially 1000 times faster; lower time lags in transmitting signals; and lower cost and energy use. The overall effect is that vastly more data can be utilised. The significance of 5G is that it can enable other technologies to function much more effectively: self-drive cars, remote driving and automated traffic management; virtual reality; drones; remote surgery; and the many applications of Artificial Intelligence. The much faster speeds also facilitate rapid data transfer which is the key to the so-called Internet of Things connecting numerous everyday objects to the Internet.

Hostility to Huawei in the USA has been building up over the years instigated by competitors and latterly by the federal government. Accusations have been several: espionage, for which there is scant evidence; stealing technology which may once have been true but is less likely since it is ahead of its competitors; potential espionage by creating a 'back door' into Western networks which is possible but preventable; and exceptional levels of state financial support which may be true in part but is true in many sectors and many countries. The underlying anxiety is that Huawei's relative success could prove cumulative, as it is able to embed its own standards across the world such that many countries become dependent on its technology. And, because a Chinese company would be the dominant provider, China would then be the main beneficiary of technologies which will drive change, productivity improvements and growth in future, just as US companies have dominated the Internet and data revolution so far.

There are numerous cases of civil and criminal cases being brought in the USA against the company, its partners and employees to disrupt its business. But the big escalation has come, in August this year in the form of new rules which ban the sale to Huawei of microchips using US technology and these are the chips which power its 5G telecoms applications, smartphones and other businesses like cloud computing and virtual reality.

Some analysts believe that the sanctions could do mortal damage to the company by stifling its smart-phone and consumer goods business. The more mainstream view is that they will inflict short-term damage but, in the longer term, China will build up an indigenous capacity in the highest quality components and Huawei will grow through its domestic market. Huawei is also switching to cloud computing where it does have access to US chips under licensing agreements which predate the export restrictions. The shift to more inward-looking technological development has big implications for other areas like AI where China is believed to be currently behind and striving to catch up. But other Chinese companies are also in the wars, as with TikTok.

TikTok Under Attack

TikTok is an altogether different proposition from Huawei. It is not involved in core telecommunications infrastructure. It is a popular video app which has enjoyed great success amongst American (and other) teenagers. President Trump has declared it to be a 'security threat' because it accumulates a large amount of data on Americans though the company claims, plausibly, that the data is not stored in China and that its activities are purely commercial and innocuous.

Nonetheless there has been an executive order that TikTok should be sold to an American company or close. India has also barred TikTok though more as a way as showing that India has the capacity to retaliate (over a border incident) by damaging Chinese economic interests. In the USA, TikTok's parent company ByteDance (founded and owned by Zhang Yiming) has been involved in preliminary talks over a sale to Microsoft, Oracle or Walmart. But the Chinese government has announced its intention of retaliating over the forced sale by imposing export controls on 'personalised information recommendation based on data analysis' (sic) which include the complex algorithms used by ByteDance and are important in AI. Indeed, AI is the next battleground.

Artificial Intelligence: the New Frontier

One crucial area in future is Artificial Intelligence which will enable closer approximation to human behaviour in such fields as visual and speech recognition and language translation and many other applications which will raise the productivity of economies which can develop and apply the technologies. The USA and China, and probably nowhere else, have the infrastructure to develop as AI industrial bases. Both have already mobilised a large research capacity and of the thousands of companies now working on AI applications approaching half are American and a quarter Chinese.

There is broad acceptance that China is some way behind. In particular US companies are further ahead in producing the advanced semi-conductors required to make the micro-chips for AI-enabled devices. And American research is also producing significantly more research papers at present and is thought to be way ahead in fundamental, theoretical, work in areas like algorithm research.

But China has some long term strengths. One, already noted above, is a capacity to generate enormous amounts of data. The big data-generating platforms – Baidu, TenCent and Ali Baba –

are involved in AI start-ups as are their American equivalents, notably Google. But in quantitative terms China has more internet users than the USA and Europe combined, and lack of privacy means that more can be harvested in China.

China also has manpower in depth. The Thousand Talents Programme, referred to earlier, is being used to mobilise highly capable, high level, scientists and potential entrepreneurs for the AI sector. It is a measure of the alarm in the USA over Chinese scientific advance that it is cutting back visas for Chinese researchers who might return to strengthen the AI programme back home

The West's response to the Chinese Technological Challenge

The US is becoming more aggressive towards the threat of Chinese technological competition as we have seen with Huawei (and TikTok). The reasoning behind it has several strands. First, there is a belief that China, like the former USSR, will crumble if forced to compete in advanced technology as in the 'star wars' of the 1980s. The argument is that, while China has been very effective in mobilising resources behind some new technologies or one or two exceptional ventures like Huawei, it has failed, so far, elsewhere – as in semiconductors – and lacks the entrepreneurial eco-system of Silicon Valley. There is however, as discussed above, a history in the West of constantly underestimating the ability of the Chinese system to adapt.

A variation of the same argument is that, as things stand, China will indeed overtake the USA with its various advantages of scale and human resources. But it is still predominantly in the process of learning and acquiring rather than defending new technological advances and is therefore not likely to retaliate against hostile moves provided that they are made now rather than later.

There has indeed been a reticence to respond strongly to the attacks on Huawei. However, the idea that China can be stopped from developing runs into the objection that, by throwing up barriers, the USA is giving China an incentive to pursue a more self-reliant strategy for acquiring what it calls 'stranglehold technologies' like semi-conductors and batteries. There has already been a big push to accelerate semiconductor development. If successful, China will then build up its own supply chains and exclude foreign collaborators to the disadvantage of the leading Western companies, like Apple and Qualcomm.

Then, it is said that there is a threat to national security' from companies like Huawei. Such arguments are difficult to prove either way since they rely on secret sources of information and trust in the judgements of the security services and the military. There is the fear that a Chinese presence embedded in a system opens the way to espionage or sabotage in the event of more serious conflict. Huawei's protestation that they have no interest whatever in spying meets the accusation that Chinese companies are not free agents but, as discussed above, required under national security legislation to act in the interests of the Chinese state.

Whilst there is a theoretical possibility that companies like Huawei could be commandeered for political purposes, and could use their expertise and integration with Western infrastructure to find a 'backdoor' into important networks connected to national security, their history is one of operational independence. In a rational world, the issue is one of quantifying and managing risk, not merely asserting or denying it; but the political momentum behind a 'cold war' makes such nuanced judgements difficult, as the British government discovered when it had to abandon its carefully calibrated approach to Huawei in the face of US sanctions.

Third, there are issues around the collection of data and how it is collected. The case against companies like TikTok has not been that the data they collect is militarily important or strategic – comic sketches and snatches of music are hardly that – but that vast amounts of data on individuals collected through social media is transferred to China. It isn't clear why American teenagers should be more concerned about their data being stored in China than non-American teenagers should be concerned about Facebook data being collected in California; but, to the extent that the location of storage and data use is a concern, it can be made a condition of operation. Moreover, the Chinese companies concerned have claimed that they do not, nor have any interest in, transferring data to China and antagonising their customers.

In reality, the driver behind the more aggressive approach to China has little to do with national security in a narrow sense. Its basis is a fear that China is catching up (as in AI) or already ahead (as with 5G) in the new foundation technologies which will, in turn, lead to the higher productivity and growth which will further strengthen China's position as the world's leading economy. And once a position of technological leadership is secured, the rest of the world finds it cheaper and easier to adopt the standards of the leading player. And that in turn will strengthen China's influence relative to the West and the USA in particular which is more or less troubling depending on one's view of Chinese intentions.

Chapter 5.

Is China Expansionist?

Much of the current hostility towards China is backed up by the assertion that China, and particularly its current President, are 'expansionist', striving to expand both frontiers and influence in Asia and also globally. Territorial expansion and influence are however not the same thing and the second may be true but not the first. And an important distinction also needs to be made between being assertive around the defence and consolidation of uncertain and insecure national boundaries and wider aspirations of domination which, in China's case, have scant basis.

History As A Guide

There is a pessimistic argument amongst students of international relations that the emergence of new 'superpowers' is bound to lead to conflict as the newcomer asserts itself and the incumbent fights back. The theory is described as the Thucydides Trap because of the way Athens and Sparta demonstrated this particular dynamic. There are many similar cases in history but others which don't follow the script (Portugal and Spain; the UK and the USA).

In modern times Germany and Japan sought empires and overseas territory leading to war. Conflict between the USA (with NATO) and the USSR almost came to nuclear blows but they fought a mostly peaceful Cold War instead.

China was on the receiving end of Western expansion as when its 19th Century weakness resulted in humiliating military defeat in the two Opium Wars and the 'unequal treaties' governing trade with Britain and other European countries. And it is that history which fuels much of the nationalism in today's China. But when Chinese dynasties were very powerful and, indeed, had a strong navy as when Chinese ships reached Africa and visited the Middle East and India, they showed little interest in acquiring colonies or dependent territories overseas.

That is not to say that China has been leading a pacifist existence. It has fought numerous wars over the centuries with its neighbours - Vietnam, Korea, Burma and Japan- and most recently with Vietnam and India. But only where border issues are unsettled, as with India in the Himalayas, has China used force to pursue its claims. Warriors do not figure in China's gallery of heroes. It is difficult to identify a Chinese Napoleon or Wellington or Saladin or Caesar or Alexander.

But what about the China Sea?

Critics of Chinese expansionism point to the modern history of acquiring, and militarising, small islands and atolls, including reclaimed land in the South China Sea, mainly in the Paracel and Sprattly islands far from the Chinese mainland.

The Chinese argue that they are in good company; the other countries in the region – Vietnam, the Philippines and Malaysia – also have territorial claims, sometimes overlapping. These arguments have rumbled on for years but the balance of argument changed with a clear legal ruling in an international court that China is legally in the wrong to interpret the Law of the Sea as permitting states to claim 12 mile territorial waters around reclaimed rocks and islets; rather, the waters are international. The US navy has used aggressive patrolling to assert that principle.

For their part, the Chinese have no incentive to disrupt international sea-lanes which they use more than any other country. In any event, for Europeans, a much more serious and relevant problem is the maritime dispute between Greece and Turkey where Turkey has adopted the Chinese view of territoriality.

The Taiwanese Anomaly

The one clear case where China threatens military aggression is Taiwan. Every Chinese leader since the Revolution in 1949 has seen the restoration of Taiwan to China as fundamental principle, returning territory which was taken in a war with Japan in 1894/5. President Xi is no different from his predecessors in making a 'red line' of this issue.

The issue is, of course, not new and since the Nixon/Kissinger reconciliation in 1972 the USA has accepted in principle that Taiwan is part of China. But it has also supported and defended Taiwan's de facto independence including defence sales. China has in practice been highly pragmatic, welcoming Taiwanese tourists and big Taiwanese investors (such as Foxconn).

The worry is that a formal move to legitimise Taiwanese independence, supported by the United States, would be regarded by China as a provocation leading to potential conflict. This issue has been carefully managed for half a century and the danger of a new Cold War is that it could spill over into something hotter.

The Chinese elite has a sufficiently developed sense of history and of long term trends to be able to recognise the significance of India's economic rise as well as China's own. On purchasing power measures, India is now the world's third largest economy-about 40% the size of China- and will soon overtake China as the most populous country. Despite many obstacles and often dysfunctional democratic government, India is one of the world's fastest growing economies. Yet China's current quarrel with India over an uninhabitable, remote, corner of the Himalayas, broadening out into Indian economic sanctions against it, is one China could do without, given the rift with the USA. The old adage about not fighting a war on two fronts is apposite.

An adversarial relationship with India has evolved from several causes. The first was the legacy of colonialism. India became independent and China experienced Communist revolution at almost the same time (1947 and 1949 respectively). Both new regimes inherited a long, disputed, frontier essentially defined by British colonial authorities and complicated by the fact that parts of Kashmir in the border area were occupied by Pakistan. Lack of resolution led to a war in 1962 when India was trounced by the Chinese army leading to some boundary revision in China's favour but a continued stand-off elsewhere.

Then, both India and China became thermo-nuclear powers and see each other as potentially hostile. Third, and linked to the previous point, China has allied itself with Pakistan which has fought three serious wars with India and has a continuing dispute over the future of Kashmir.

China has become a significant force in Pakistan's development through the Belt-and-Road initiative and now has a direct road route through Tibet and Pakistan to the Arabian Sea and a major naval base at Gardar: all of which India considers threatening. And fourth, India has been gradually moving away from its traditional close ties to the USSR, then Russia, and towards the USA.

A common belief in democracy; links with India's diaspora in the USA; and India's increasingly sophisticated and strong economy and burgeoning IT sector: these have brought America and India together. Indian Prime Minister Modi has forged close links with Trump personally.

In that context the punch-up in the Himalayas between Indian and Chinese troops, fought mostly with fists and sticks rather than guns, escalated from being a minor episode to a major incident. The 20 or so Indian casualties were treated as military heroes and India retaliated, not militarily but economically. India banned over100 Chinese apps including TikTok and WeChat as well as telecommunications equipment from Huawei and ZTE. Indian consumers have been urged to boycott Chinese goods.

Since Chinese exports to India are four times its imports from India, the scope for Chinese retaliation is very limited and the same companies being hit in the USA are being hit again in India, and excluded from what is potentially a huge market. Most serious in the longer term, India has been enlisted into the new Cold War on America's side with little American effort.

Belt and Road: New Marshall Plan or Neo-colonialism?

One of President Xi's personal initiatives is an ambitious global infrastructure initiative, the Belt and Road Initiative (BRI). Over 70 countries have subscribed to it with varying commitment and enthusiasm though there is outright hostility from the USA and India. Other countries have mixed feelings, seeing the undoubted benefits in improved infrastructure but also the costs of finance and other ties to China.

The concept is visionary: re-establishing or improving the communications once enjoyed along the over-land silk routes from the Far East to Europe (the belt) and the maritime sea routes via the Indian Ocean, and Africa, to Europe (the road). The land routes, in particular, open up communications which have long been closed or difficult, though Russia and Central Asia. A generous view of the initiative is that it potentially adds greatly to physical connectivity and development around the proposed infrastructure. In support there is a well- financed multilateral infrastructure bank (the AIIB) which has the UK – but not the USA – amongst its shareholders.

Apart from influence and 'soft power', the BRI brings some tangible benefits to China: export markets, access to raw materials, greater use of the yuan/renminbi; and better economic integration of its own underdeveloped, and unsettled, regions like Xinjiang.

The vision is long-term. The BRI started in 2013 and is due to be completed in 2049. Already, several countries have built deep-water ports or major road and rail projects. Progress has been disrupted by the pandemic but a bigger threat is the negative reaction of some of the countries which are part of the BRI, such as Malaysia, and which have queried the cost of the loans and other conditions. It will be a major test of Chinese leadership as to whether it can show sufficient flexibility to make the BRI a development success story and a good illustration of China's peaceful intentions rather than more grist to the mill of the new Cold War.

China: how big a military threat?

The sense that China is a 'threat' often relates to growing Chinese military capability and potential. China's spending on defence has been rising rapidly, in line with the economy, and the use of technology is of growing sophistication. But it is difficult to make the case that China has anything remotely resembling a capacity to fight the USA, or pursue disputes beyond its borders..

The most recent figures have China spending just under 2% of its GNP on defence, and that after a decade of 10% growth (from an era when Deng and his immediate successors regarded defence as wasteful and an impediment to development). At 2019 levels of spending and at market exchange rates China's military budget is 40% of America's. But a $60,000 US salary would buy several PLA equivalents; though equipment can reasonably be valued at world prices.

If corrected in this way the China budget is roughly 75% of the US and on the same basis the Indian defence budget is 40% of US levels and Russia's 30%.

China outranks the US only in one- largely irrelevant- area: numbers of troops, with 2.3 million versus 1.3 million and 8 million reservists versus 800,000. But the Chinese government is trying to cut numbers, recognising that quality trumps quantity. And, there, China is at a big disadvantage. Whilst American troops are highly trained, based on recent combat experience (Iraq; Afghanistan), China last fought a war 40 years ago against the battle hardened Vietnamese and suffered a humiliating set-back.

China has a slightly higher number of tanks, though over a third are of 1950's vintage and the US has vastly bigger numbers of armoured vehicles. A lot is being made of China's expanding navy but it has 2 aircraft carriers to 20 for the USA. It has roughly a third as many aircraft and many of those are seriously dated. And while China has a nuclear weapons capability its number of warheads is around 300 as against 65,000 for the USA of which 1600 are deployed.

It is possible, of course, to imagine from China's technological prowess all manner of horror stories. The fact that Chinese missiles and space technology have led to a successful mission to the 'dark' side of the moon is being used to argue that China is planning wars in space. The fact that it has developed its own version of GPS from a Chinese satellite is being used to argue that China could be planning to disable US satellites (and, no doubt, vice versa). To the extent that dispassionate analysis shows these to be real risks, it is obviously prudent to have a deterrent capability. But these futuristic scenarios are a long way from the ground reality of inexperienced troops and ancient equipment.

Looking at the situation qualitatively rather than quantitatively, but also theoretically, the RAND Foundation judges that China's capacity to fight a conventional war with the USA near its own borders over, say, Taiwan is improving to near-parity. The USA retains a significant advantage further afield, such as the South China Sea.

On a global comparison, China isn't remotely close to parity. Unlike the USSR, which tried to match the USA militarily but neglected its economy, China has prioritised economic development and growth. Even with recent big improvements in capability, China's defence profile is consistent with its history as a country which has been military active around its borders but is not, essentially, expansionist. Its battle with the West is over ideas.

Chapter 6.

The Ideological Battle

Why Can't the Chinese Be Democrats Like Us?

A popular argument used in the West in explaining and justifying a new Cold War is that, somehow, today's Chinese leadership has let down its people and the wider world by not evolving from economic liberalisation to political liberalisation. Liberal democracy is both correct and inevitable and China should have followed (most of) Eastern Europe and some Asian countries like South Korea along the road from autocratic government to multi-party democracy with competitive elections.

This sense of disappointment, even betrayal, surfaced when President Xi extended his period in office and more recently with the crackdown on pro-democracy protestors in Hong Kong.

The Chinese have a robust reaction. Their first response is to ask: 'Why are you surprised?'. The architect of modern China, Deng Xiaoping, always made it abundantly clear that economic and political liberalisation were separate issues. His plans to open up the Chinese economy and to extend personal freedoms inside China – over foreign travel for example – did not mean an end to the monopoly in power for the Communist Party. Deng was contemptuous of Gorbachev's 'glasnost'; he described Gorbachev as a 'fool' and predicted that chaos would follow – as it did.

And he never disowned his personal responsibility for the massacre in Tiananmen Square in 1989 following the introduction of martial law to curb violent unrest. His successors developed a more collegiate, less personalised, leadership style, until Xi, but never entertained a Western-style, multi-party democracy. 'Reformers' look to successful 'democracies' like Singapore where elections reinforce indefinite one-party rule and dissent is carefully controlled.

There is also, as the Chinese point out, some irony in the fact that growing Western disapproval of Chinese governance coincides with a decline in the prevalence of 'liberal democracy' elsewhere. Former 'democracies' have reverted to autocratic systems of government without losing their status in democratic clubs like the EU (Hungary) or Western alliances (Turkey).

Some formerly robust democratic systems like India have developed 'strong-man' leadership styles, eroding civil liberties. In the USA itself the President openly canvasses the idea of staying in power even if he loses an election and presides over a corrupted plutocracy in which a handful of very rich individuals have disproportionate power. So what, the Chinese ask, is the democratic alternative to Communist-ruled China?

Is there an alternative?

The argument from the Chinese regime would be that there is a wide continuum of political systems, with varying degrees of public participation in the choice of government and toleration of dissent, reflecting national histories and circumstances. Its supporters will say that there has never been, as there has been in most western countries, a long history of democratic institution building.

Modern China emerged from a century of 'chaos' and civil war (including the period under Mao) and the public places a high premium on stability and security. In the absence of free elections it is difficult to know if this is a correct statement of public opinion or merely self-serving. There are surveys carried out by Pew, or the Edelman Trust Barometer, which suggest that the public has far more trust in the government in China (over 80%) than in the UK or USA (under 40%). Moreover the Chinese system does appear to accommodate a good deal of individual dissent (provided it is not organised and part of a movement). Localised, non-political, protests over pay and working conditions or land rights or corrupt officials are widespread.

There is a defence of the Chinese system that their model is not merely good for China but good for the world. It provides a 'public good'. It keeps populism in check and specifically the nationalism and rage about foreign mis-deeds which may be lurking just below the surface. Such restraint, it is argued, has made possible the development of working relations, mainly around commerce, with Japan despite the atrocities of the War. And it has enabled good relations, so far, with Western countries responsible for the 'century of humiliation'.

The Chinese can argue that some of the most dangerous relationships in the world right now are fuelled by public opinion in antagonistic democracies: Israel and Iran; Greece and semi-democratic Turkey; India and Pakistan. In China, such passions are managed.

The 'public good' argument is also used to argue that, under stable Communist Party leadership, China is able to play a constructive role in tackling global issues through multilateral agreements governing pandemics, climate change, economic development or trade. Chinese propaganda contrasts the constructive role of China with the disruptive, populist, 'America First' policies of the Trump administration (or with the UK and Brexit).

It is right to be sceptical about China's actual performance in these areas, as opposed to its claims, but at least it is a cheerleader for long term cooperation rather than being a disruptor. And implicit in this argument is the sense that China's leadership is essentially conservative – as supporters of a stable status quo – rather than a revolutionary power or a wrecking ball in the manner of Putin or Trump.

But what about the minorities?

A particular criticism of today's China is the lack of tolerance for religious and other, culturally defined, minorities. The current concerns are over the Uighurs of Xinjiang, and some shocking accounts have emerged. In the past, the Tibetans have also experienced brutal attacks on their identity.

The Chinese authorities' response is that they have no problem with accommodating religions, as such, and do so with Christians, Muslims and others; nor do they discriminate on grounds of ethnicity, there being many people who are not Han Chinese but are peacefully integrated.

A problem arises when minority groups seek a degree of 'self-determination' up to and including political independence. There is a long-standing tension in many countries between demands from minorities for self-determination and 'territorial integrity': the assertion of a majority view that states have to defend themselves against secession and disintegration.

The Chinese take an uncompromising stand on 'territorial integrity' based on its long history of unsettled borders, foreign intervention and rebellion. They point to the risks of bloody break-up (Yugoslavia; Ethiopia; Georgia; Bangladesh; Sudan) and that they are far from alone in using force to assert their 'territorial integrity': Kashmir and India; Kurdistan and Turkey; various in Myanmar. Even Western democracies have struggled to manage demands for 'self- determination' peacefully within the democratic process, as in Spain.

However tragic the position of the Uighurs and Tibetans and however harsh the Chinese government's behaviour, Western governments have tacitly accepted that 'Chinese sovereignty' has to be respected and that this is an internal matter for China. Indeed, President Trump is said (by his National Security

Advisor, John Bolton) to have told President Xi that he had no objections to raise in connection with the Chinese treatment of the Uighurs.

But, unlike President Trump, there are many who see a fundamental divide with China over 'liberal values' and 'human rights' and who do not see values as constrained by 'sovereignty'. This is especially so as the new Cold War against China is bringing together a wide political coalition from those, on the political 'right', who see the emerging conflict as a continuation from the last Cold war against Communism, to liberals and social democrats, who feel the need to make a statement on 'human rights'.

And business now has to contend with ethical institutional investors and bad publicity for alleged 'complicity' in human rights abuses: Disney for using Xinjiang as a backcloth to a recent film and HSBC for acting as an apologist for the authorities in Hong Kong. China is far from being the only country, or the worst, when it comes to human rights abuses, but the issue adds another dimension to the Cold War.

The Different Meanings of Human Rights

No Chinese would seek to argue that they are against 'human rights'. But they tend to mean something different. The Chinese stress economic and social rights: the elimination of absolute poverty, literacy and access to education, for girls as well as boys, access to health services and reduced mortality. These are all areas where China has demonstrated big advances, a product both of economic growth and a government which has given priority to them.

By contrast, the Western view of human rights emphasises freedom of speech and of the press, freedom from persecution of individual dissidents and minorities, fair trials, democratic political processes and judicial independence. In an ideal world both sets of rights would be supported and advance together. European social democracies come closest to that ideal.

Some countries in the developing world have tried to reconcile and promote both. India is perhaps the most important example but it has lagged behind China in advancing economic and social rights and is currently losing its halo in respect of wider civil and political rights. But China's poor record on the latter, and seeming indifference to it, has now come to a head in the unrest in Hong Kong and the Chinese reaction to it.

Hong Kong: One Country, One System?

The political upheaval in Hong Kong in the last year has been a major catalyst polarising opinion internationally for and against China. Until that happened, the peaceful and orderly management of the hand-over of the British colony had been a success story and reflected very well on both the Chinese and British governments. Hong Kong had become a British colony as a result of 'unequal treaties' in the 19th Century and owed much to adventurers who exploited China economically and particularly through the opium trade.

It would have been very understandable if the Chinese had simply annexed Hong Kong, backed by military force, in the way that India did with the remnants of the Portuguese empire, Indonesia with former Dutch territory and Morocco with Spanish Sahara. However, they insisted on due legal process and took over when the colony's lease formally expired. The motives may have been hard headed: to preserve intact the successful capitalist economy of Hong Kong. But China also wanted to send out a message that it could be trusted to honour legal obligations, even if obtained by dubious and unfair means.

Under the Basic Law agreed with Britain – a national law of China replacing the colonial constitution, but with the status of an international treaty – there was to be a pro-longed transitional period until 2047 and full integration with the P.R.C. In the meantime, the principle of 'one country, two systems' would apply.

For 22 years the arrangement worked effectively and without undue controversy. Chinese territorial integrity and sovereignty was acknowledged – the 'one country' – along with a degree of self-determination in the form of legal safeguards for freedom of assembly and speech which do not apply elsewhere in China – the 'two systems'.

But it was too good to last

Last year, the Chief Minister, Carrie Lam, proposed a new extradition agreement which would enable Hong Kong residents to be extradited to face trial on the mainland. There were massive protest demonstrations by those who feared the move would erode Hong Kong's relative legal autonomy. The demonstrations may also have owed something to frustration over the acute scarcity of affordable housing, a failing of both the colonial administration and its pro-Beijing successor. And perhaps even more important were the underlying anxieties of a younger generation, fearful that they would have no long term future when Hong Kong finally merges into the PRC. The administration clearly misjudged the public mood and capitulated in the face of the protests.

But the demonstrations did not stop. And, although overwhelmingly peaceful, there was some violence, including attacks with petrol bombs on the police. The demands of the protestors escalated including demands for fuller democratic rights and, from some, for independence.

It is far from clear what the demonstrators hoped to achieve by backing the Chinese authorities into a corner. Continued massive demonstrations represented a breakdown of order and an attack on the 'one nation'. Under the Basic Law there are powers to use the 6000 troops deployed in the territory in an emergency. But the Chinese regime stayed its hand calculating, no doubt correctly, that for troops to shoot demonstrators in the streets could incite a wider conflict.

Leading to draconian security measures

In the event it chose to use legal means, rather than force, through the draconian National Security Law. The powers of the new Law included widely defined political offences: sedition, subversion, terrorism and collusion with foreign powers. 'Complex' cases can be tried in China. The law can also be applied extra-territorially to offences committed outside Hong Kong. The new law has already led to the arrests of some democratic campaigners and the establishment of tighter control over the media and freedom of expression and the judiciary. But it achieved its immediate objective of clearing the streets without bloodshed.

There has been almost universal condemnation of the new Chinese law and China has received little credit for relative restraint. The severity of the provisions sweep away much of what was distinctive about Hong Kong under the 'two systems'. But, to keep some perspective, Hong Kong isn't and never has been a democracy; the British colonial authorities did not allow voters to choose their Governor.

Under the Basic Law there is an 'ultimate aim' of universal suffrage to choose the Chief Minister but, in the meantime, the Legislative Council is dominated by appointments, mostly commercial special interests. Democracy has been allowed in elections to largely powerless local councils (for which pro-democracy candidates swept the board last November) and latterly, in primary elections, to choose some members of the Legco. The new law seems, however, likely to snuff out any really independent political expression.

Temporary or permanent?

It remains to be seen whether the new crackdown is a permanent change in status with a disappearance not just of limited democratic freedoms but also of robust debate in the media and of courts free from political interference. Judicial independence is crucial since it is arguably the most valuable, distinctive, asset of Hong Kong. Pessimists claim that Hong Kong will now become simply part of the mainland and subject to the recent, more severe, tightening of Communist Party rule.

What was to happen in 2047 starts now. Optimists (and there aren't too many) believe that the Law has been designed to restore order and that, once it is and people the Chinese authorities regard as 'trouble-makers' have been removed from circulation, Hong Kong will revert to much of its previous 'normal'. For those who can avoid dabbling in 'secession, subversion, terrorism or collusion with foreign powers' life will continue as normal.

Either way, it is clear that the original 'two systems' concept has largely gone. There is also a polarisation of international opinion followed by sanctions. The UK has suspended its extradition treaty with Hong Kong, imposed an arms embargo on material which could be used for 'internal repression' (by the police) and offered to establish a 'route to citizenship' for the 3 million Hong Kong holders of 'British national overseas' passports.

A smarter Chinese government might have called the British bluff on immigration but it reacted with outrage to what it saw as an attack on its sovereignty. More seriously, the US administration introduced sanctions against specific individuals judged to be 'extinguishing Chinese freedoms' and financial institutions doing business with them and has ceased to treat Hong Kong as separate from China for trade. purposes.

Which raises questions over economic impacts

Much will now depend on how the disorder, the Chinese reaction and the Western sanctions combine to affect China's future as a major financial centre: indeed, Asia's foremost business hub.

First reactions are that business can now continue as normal. The Hang Seng index and stock turnover have risen. Hong

Kong continues to offer Chinese companies freedom from government controls on capital movements and a market to raise capital internationally. For the 1500 international firms which have established their regional headquarters in the territory there remains, for the moment, a big pool of professional- legal and accounting- expertise and a favourable, if expensive, business environment with an independent legal system and free circulation of information.

But there are potential threats from the new Security Law in relation to commercial matters. Economic reporting and analysis which is unfavourable to China or highlights negative trends might be deemed unacceptable. The courts may no longer be credibly independent if one of the litigants has powerful political connections in main-land China or if fraud trials seem designed to protect favoured individuals.

The big data companies, like Facebook, which can currently operate in Hong Kong but not in China may encounter 'national security' issues. Some financial institutions may find themselves trapped between US sanctions and Chinese Security Law: that, if they comply with one, they break the other. HSBC has already suffered reputational damage outside China for endorsing the new Law in Hong Kong.

It remains to be seen whether international business is ultimately more influenced by the new law or by the restoration of order. 40% of the 1500 members of the American Chamber of Commerce in Hong Kong have said they plan to move assets or operations out of Hong Kong. But there is no sign yet of any flagging appetite for IPO money, more of which has been raised in Hong Kong this year than in New York or Nasdaq- with a massive Ant Group public offering planned.

It is plausible to imagine that a lot of Hong Kong's strengths, like legal arbitration in commercial disputes, could leak away to competing centres, notably Singapore. International business, seeking a hub for their Asian regional operations, and seeing the politicisation of the courts and day-to-day life and the effect on their local employees, will quietly slip away too.

The most likely beneficiary is Singapore which is ironic since Singapore isn't exactly the epitome of lively, critical, democratic politics. The tragedy for Hong Kong could be that Beijing doesn't care all that much. Shanghai is already replacing Hong Kong as the leading capital market for Chinese business and as a business hub with cheaper property and purpose-built infrastructure. There is little doubt that the Chinese want a more constrained Hong Kong to succeed in its traditional business role; but they will not be unduly disadvantaged if it does not.

Chapter 7

The Making of the New Cold War

There is little doubt that over the last few years, and certainly within the few months since the Covid epidemic, there has been a hardening of attitudes towards China in Western and some other major countries like India: a shift in the balance from the optimists who envisage and welcome continuing 'engagement' to the pessimists who see China as a growing 'threat'. The shift is most palpable and significant in the USA.

I will review the reasons for this shift before looking at how different countries are responding. The reasons vary a great deal, and are often contradictory, but they have all fed into generalised suspicion or hostility or fear.

The first factor is the worry is that China has acquired great influence and leverage as a result of its overtaking the USA to become the world's biggest economy, with the potential to widen the gap as its living standards approach US levels. There is however a division amongst the China critics between those who believe that the politics of an authoritarian Communist state are not compatible with a market economy (and so China, like the Soviet Union, will fail) and those who believe Chinese 'state capitalism' is providing highly competent government (and so China is to be feared).

The latter view is gaining ascendency.

Within that big picture, there are numerous grievances about 'unfair' trading practices: President Trump's obsession with bilateral trade deficits; supposed exchange rate manipulation; subsidies enjoyed by state enterprises; active industrial policy;

conditions imposed on foreign companies in China; and longstanding complaints about intellectual property theft.

Most of these however are longstanding issues arising from China's progression from a poor, planned, economy to a developed market economy.

Some, like the exchange rate issue, are long gone and others (as with intellectual property rights) are certainly improving. But there is a real issue of substance: the lack of an effective framework of rules to anchor a 'state capitalist' superpower.

Then there is technology

The complaint used to be that China was (or is) copying or stealing technology. Now the concern is more that China is ahead (telecommunications) or might soon be (AI).

Amongst the worries on the Western side are that technological capability will open up possibilities for espionage and cyber-warfare and that it will strengthen China's military capability; but these can be countered and ring-fenced directly.

Then there are the specific interests of the leading US data companies-notably Facebook and Google-which are largely excluded from China by the Great Firewall while they face Chinese competition elsewhere including in the USA.

Perhaps the most potent concern is that, if China achieves parity or superiority in core new technologies, it will then be able to dictate the standards that the world uses.

With martial behaviour and language

There are also those who argue that China is a military threat. However, China, even with its enhanced capability, isn't a direct threat to the USA (let alone Europe which has the much bigger problem of Russia on its doorstep and the instability of the Middle East and Eastern Mediterranean).

There is no plausible Pearl Harbour scenario.

There is a specific threat to Taiwan, and long has been, and that is an issue for the USA and its defence guarantees as also with the various longstanding territorial disputes with China's neighbours, mostly in and around the South China Sea. Armed conflict remains improbable but other aspects of defence, like cyber-security, have more substance. And what matters is the perception of conflict, however well grounded.

Perceptions of enmity have been fanned by aggressive expressions of Chinese nationalism matching that of Trump in the USA. There has been a distinct change of tone in Chinese diplomacy exemplified by the 'wolf warriors' who spout the kind of propaganda normally associated with states like North Korea.

A variety of governments – the UK, Australia, India, Canada, Japan, Korea, the Philippines – have caused offence by being critical of China's internal policies, including in Hong Kong, or being too friendly to Taiwan or in some other way, leading to a dressing down and some form of punitive action. We may regard some of this behaviour as petulant and alienating but that doesn't make it a threat. Nor is it clear if the Party leadership is manipulating and stirring up nationalist feeling or trying to manage it. Nonetheless the switch from banalities to belligerence is fuelling the hostility.

And the clash of values

What adds fuel to the fire is the self-righteous assertion from the West of moral superiority and insistence that the values of 'liberal democracy' must prevail, usually coupled with expressions of regret that China has 'failed' by not liberalising politically. But it was naïve to believe that political liberalisation would follow economic liberalisation when Deng and his economic reformers made it clear that it would not happen.

And there is a world of difference between the anarchic, revolutionary violence of Mao's era and the harsh but

70

competent technocracy of today (which also allows freedom of travel). Many of the educated Chinese elite will now argue, moreover, that democracy is what is discredited as a system – witness Trump and Brexit – and that their system is simply better.

Western governments have ignored these political differences in the past and got on with business. What now makes that more difficult, especially in Europe, is the role of civil society in fanning anger over 'human rights' abuse.

The abuse is real enough in places like Xinjiang and Tibet. But that is true in other countries which are allied to the USA and UK and it is arguable that many Western politicians don't share 'liberal values' either, including the President of the USA (though that may change in a Democrat administration).

These issues matter, however, since they have helped form an unholy alliance against China, between the right-wing 'hawks' who are still 'fighting Communism' and the liberal and social democratic left. As the Hong Kong crisis unfolded, both sides competed in condemnation.

The other recent event which has crystallised hostility has been Covid. A great deal of ill-will was created by the revelation that the Chinese authorities were initially responsible for the growing spread of Covid and specifically that the secretive nature of the Communist Party apparatus prevented early warnings reaching the outside world. Subsequently the Chinese authorities did a remarkable job in containing the disease.

China has been much more effective than big democracies like the US, India and Brazil in stopping its spread and politicians like Trump have used China as a scapegoat for their own failures. Nonetheless the pandemic has left a legacy of distrust of dependency on China generally and in particular on supply chains.

The charge sheet is long and contains some points which are valid in whole or part. The main Chinese response is: you may not like us or our system but we are not a threat to you and are not trying to run the world; but we expect to be treated with respect reflecting our position as a great power and an economic superpower. There are potential allies and supporters on both sides.

Chapter 8

The Line-up in the New Cold War

I have discussed at length the hardening position of the United States. What is striking is the shift in public opinion. According to Pew Research, ten years ago Americans' view of China was strongly positive. Three years ago 'favourable' and 'unfavourable' views were roughly the same. Now, roughly four times as many people have an unfavourable view. The Covid pandemic and President Trump's trade war appear to be key factors. Pew surveys in Europe are showing a similar shift; across Europe, half say that their opinion of China has deteriorated in the last year.

Mixed Feelings in the EU

The European Union is torn. Its members have different views on China and different interests and the UK, which had a central role on the Hong Kong issue, has left. Unlike the USA, no European country has a direct interest in the defence and security issues of the region though concerns over human rights are probably stronger in Europe than the USA. There are also major economic interests: some positive, based on exports; some negative, based on fear of Chinese competition. The EU has declared China to be a 'systemic rival' though it isn't clear what that means.

Germany has a unique position as a big manufacturing exporter to China. There is longstanding German role in capital goods exports but the big growth has been of motor vehicle exports: $27 bn. in 2019, a growth from $3 bn. in 2005. Audi, Daimler, BMW and the rest have found Germany to be a gold mine. Overall, China is one of Germany's biggest trade partners, comparable to the USA, and Germany accounts for over 40% of EU exports to China. And there are over 5000 firms with production facilities in China.

Chancellor Merkel has seen China as a major German priority, having visited it 12 times as Chancellor, largely for trade promotion reasons, though she also values Chinese cooperation on global public goods like climate change. But she has come under attack in Germany for not speaking out more on human rights issues. And there is some disenchantment in German business over doing business in China: the requirements to transfer technology or form joint ventures. Germany post-Merkel, may well harden its position especially if a new American President invokes Western solidarity.

France also has a nuanced view. President Macron is very quiet on Chinese internal politics and France values the opportunity to sell aircraft and luxury goods to China. But France is more protectionist than most and apprehensive about Chinese competition in the high tech field. Macron is thought to be the driving force for measures to screen Chinese investment, to curb subsidised Chinese companies and to close off public procurement to Chinese companies where there is no 'reciprocity'. France dropped Huawei from its telecommunications infrastructure, like Britain, but without any fuss.

The major EU country closest to China is **Italy** which signed a Belt and Road contract. At a time when the EU was refusing help to Italy to deal with its deep economic problems, aggravated by Covid, Chinese solidarity was a powerful and appreciated signal. But the subsequent agreement of an EU support package which crosses previous red lines on debt underwriting, may have pulled Italy back into the fold.

China has lavished more attention on **Eastern European** countries several of whom have signed up to contracts under the BRI though there isn't much sign of large-scale Chinese investment yet. And there is a division of opinion. The Czech Republic has recently infuriated China by a provocative ministerial visit to Taiwan. The biggest East European enthusiasts for China, like Serbia, are currently outside the EU.

Britain loses the glow of the Golden Era

Britain has travelled a long way politically from the 'golden era' of Sino-British relations under the Coalition government. Chinese investment in Britain was, then, actively solicited and major opportunities were pursued for British exports to China in financial services, advanced manufactures, creative industries and education, all against the background of goodwill and expressions of hope.

The diplomacy helped and the symbolism of top-level political (and royal) endorsement meant a lot to China after the long history of imperial intervention. Trade has boomed (up from £10 to £80 bn. since the turn of the century). A recent survey suggested 150,000 British jobs are now based on exports of goods and services to China. Jaguar Land Rover now has a fifth of its sales in China. HSBC and Standard Charter Bank make over half their profits in China/Hong Kong.

A visible sign of the Golden Era in Britain was the inward investment by Chinese companies, They took stakes in or acquired some well-known consumer brands (Pizza Express, Weetabix, Odeon Cinemas, London black cab taxis and a couple of Premier League football sides – Southampton and Wolves) as well as the property investor Logicor, Sunseeker Yachts, the defence company Gardner Aerospace, the data company Global Switch and chip designer Imagination Technologies (the last of these being blocked on security grounds).

By far the biggest commitment was by China General Nuclear (a company blacklisted in the USA) to be a junior partner in the Hinkley Point power station alongside the French EDF. It has already invested £3.5 billion and it hopes to move on to another reactor – Bradwell – to showcase its own reactor technology.

There is, now, a move led by Conservative MPs, and backed by the Trump administration, to block Chinese investment in nuclear power. But it is difficult to see what – other than a generalised antipathy to the Chinese – the problem is. In any event, is difficult to see how it can be stopped without scuppering the whole nuclear programme very expensively if CNG walked away from Hinkley, at the cost of crippling the decarbonisation programme. Nuclear is a major headache to come.

But Huawei is today's headache

Until recently Huawei had an excellent relationship with the UK. It was involved in some of the most intimate work on British government surveillance technology at GCHQ. The security services were satisfied that it was a reliable partner and that any security risk was manageable. 5G would be more challenging but also more of an opportunity for the UK given Huawei's technological lead over other companies.

The government of Theresa May negotiated a compromise whereby Huawei was excluded from the most sensitive 'core' but welcome to operate elsewhere in the network. This perfectly sensible and acceptable compromise did not, however, last very long once the USA barred Huawei altogether, It would be impossible for Huawei to operate without switching from US to Chinese components which the security services judged could not be done safely. The government decided it had no choice but to follow the USA. It has now agreed to remove Huawei from the telecoms network. A likely consequence is that Britain will now slip from being one of the leaders in applying 5G technology to one of the laggards.

There is another legacy of the 'golden era' in the form of large numbers of Chinese students. There were roughly 126,000 last year as against 342,000 in total from outside the EU (and 27,000 from India). The numbers have been growing rapidly and, for some universities, the fee income from Chinese students keeps them financially viable. Chinese students, like Chinese tourists, also tend to spend generously in university towns. If the Chinese students were to be stopped or discouraged by the new Cold War there would be severe repercussions for the future viability of British universities.

The British government is in a bind. It wants Chinese business: trade, investment, students. But it is historically very close to the USA on political and security matters. The 'Special Relationship' will always trump the 'Golden Era'. And the UK is desperate for a post-Brexit trade agreement with the USA which precludes causing serious offence in Washington. Seven years ago the UK defied the USA when it joined the China-backed Asian Infrastructure investment Bank. It is very unlikely to do so again.

Other factors have dimmed the appeal of a 'golden era'. The Chinese saw the UK as a 'gateway to the EU'. Brexit greatly surprised the Chinese and made the UK seem an unreliable and less useful partner. On the UK side, the prospect of rich pickings for the City of London has receded with currency convertibility having receded in the short run. The Hong Kong crisis, and Britain's offer of rights to 3 million Hong Kongers has now put the political relationship into cold storage for the foreseeable future.

China's Asian Neighbours Not Spoiling for a Fight

China's near-neighbours may have good reason to be fearful of being dominated by China. But, by the same token, they depend on China economically and have to tread carefully.

Japan has a bad history with China due to the atrocities of the Japanese occupation during the War which is still invoked at times of stress. Also the war left Japan with a largely pacifist constitution and not in a position to deploy military force; it depends heavily for defence on the USA. Yet China disputes Japanese ownership of the uninhabited Senkaku/Dionyu islands which are a constant flashpoint while the more nationalist Chinese dispute Japanese ownership of Okinawa with its large American base. In economic terms however Japan depends heavily on China for exports (more than to the USA) and numerous Japanese companies invest in China.

Japan has a difficult balancing act. It needs to have a cordial relationship with China, especially on economic matters, without becoming subservient. It also relies on close economic links and military protection from the USA. Mr Abe, the long serving Prime Minister, who has just retired, somehow managed to cultivate both President Xi and President Trump. What he also did was to develop a loose trading alliance with democratic Asia-Pacific countries such as India, Korea and Australia but excluding China. The Trump administration, foolishly and petulantly, refused to join (because President Obama had supported it and also because it threatened freer trade). Trump also snubbed Japan by imposing tariffs on its exports. Trump seemed unable to grasp that Japan is an ally but will not enlist to fight a crude, aggressive, Cold War against China, especially on economic matters. But it will welcome non-confrontational friendships which help to rebalance its dependence on the Chinese superpower.

South Korea's problems are similar. Having a successful economy, and having successfully evolved from dictatorship to democracy, South Korea should be a natural recruit for any alliance of the like-minded against China. America was, after all, responsible for its creation after the war and during the Korean War and has long-standing defence ties. But South Korea has to tread warily. It is heavily dependent on China holding in check the unstable leadership of North Korea which poses an existential threat to the South. And, like Japan, its companies have major interests in China.

Other countries in the region have up and down relations with China: **Singapore** usually up, **Vietnam** usually down (but a Communist country is a doubtful ally for the West in an alliance of democrats); **Pakistan** and **Sri Lanka** up, **India** down. Several countries in the South China Sea have a territorial dispute with China. The **Philippines** was temporarily brought onside but has since annoyed Beijing and been penalised with a boycott of banana exports. **Malaysia** is unfriendly but conscious of its Chinese ethnic minority. **Thailand** and **Myanmar** have better relations with China (under military dominated governments) and **Cambodia** is a long-standing ally. **Indonesia** has received a lot of Chinese loans but is unlikely to come out on China's side in a wider confrontation. **Australia** is very dependent on China for trade but is also a key member of the Western '5 Eyes' alliance based on intelligence sharing. Its government has been outspoken on Huawei, Hong Kong and Covid provoking Chinese retaliation.

Russia is an obvious ally and has a complementary relationship: strong military, weak economy in Russia; strong economy, weaker military in China. The two countries support each other in the United Nations and other diplomatic forums.

They also share some- expensive and unsavoury – allies: **Syria, Iran, Venezuela**. Russia is an absolutely key component of the Belt and Road initiative. But there is a long history of suspicion: on Russia's side of Chinese economic domination; and on China's side of Russia's wild and unreliable business environment. Putin's personal link to Trump also muddies the alignments.

Further afield, China has acquired a good deal of influence as a result of its domination of some commodity markets and investment in mining and infrastructure, including within the Belt and Road Initiative. In **Latin America** it has invested heavily in economically troubled countries like Argentina and Ecuador as well as Venezuela without obvious benefit. Chile and Peru depend more on the China market but have kept their distance politically.

In **Africa** China has become by far the largest trade partner and aid donor. China has, in the process, acquired some useful allies like Ethiopia and others whose votes matter in international organisations. But, in some important countries like Nigeria, there has been a backlash against Chinese manufacturing competition and some allies have become expensive liabilities (Zimbabwe, Sudan). Amongst African politicians there is appreciation of Chinese help when the West turned its back but also an undercurrent of resentment of 'neo-colonialism' and sensitivity to some negative experiences of Chinese racism on a personal level.

Now China is under pressure to forgive a large amount of the debt which has piled up in Covid-stricken Africa and its future standing will depend on how generous it is willing, and can afford, to be.

Chapter 9

Conclusion: What is to be Done?

There are several conclusions but they can be summarised simply: GET REAL.

China isn't going away and can't be put down or ignored.

There are genuine, deep, differences but a new Iron Curtain will only widen them.

Relationships have to be based on several principles:

First, the reality is that China is already the world's largest economy, has overtaken the USA and that distance will widen in future. Technological parity is being achieved across a growing range of core technologies. Jealousy at China's economic progress is no basis for a policy; nor is denial. By contrast there are strong mutual benefits in trade and investment.

Second, China now expects to have influence and a role in international institutions and decision making reflecting its new economic importance. That is predictable and right.

Third, there are some military threats to China's immediate neighbours and some genuine security issues elsewhere-though there is a danger that concerns over 'security' slide in to paranoia. China is not trying to conquer the world and prioritises domestic economic performance where there are still many challenges, such as ageing.

Fourth, the Chinese government offers its people competent and stable but authoritarian government which appears to work for China. The Chinese model combines capitalism and continuing economic liberalisation –which continues- with tight, and tightening, political control within a one party state. 'Democracy' is not on the agenda.

Fifth and last, it is a regrettable fact that there are severe human rights abuses of individuals and minority groups in China (as there are in many countries). There is, at present, no common ground between Western countries' assertion of 'liberal values' and the Chinese response that this is 'interference' in their internal 'sovereignty'. But there are many other areas of productive cooperation.

The Schmoozing Strategy

The approach to China which has been dominant since it became clear that China was opening up economically, could be described as the SCHMOOZING strategy.

To realise the benefits from this new El Dorado – the vast China market and its low cost labour – companies will do their thing and governments will follow up with goodwill ministerial visits, effusive expressions of goodwill and promises of cooperation. The British 'golden era' is a prime example.

This approach is now being criticised as 'naïve'. It is said that too many companies and governments sold themselves too cheaply through over-eagerness for business; that the benefits in trade and investment were exaggerated; that the Chinese did not fully reciprocate market openings; that security risks were ignored; and that a 'blind eye' was turned to lack of democracy and human rights abuses in China.

Groups like the backbench China Research Group of British Conservative MPs and the Henry Jackson Society in America have majored on these criticisms, also adding an ideological note of hostility to a Communist regime.

Many of these points have a degree of truth. But the benefits in trade and investment have been very real. China has become more open and easier to do business in than other important emerging markets. It is opening its doors further to Western capital as America tries to close doors. Security risks, as with Huawei, can be and have been managed carefully, and are probably exaggerated in general. 'Blind eyes' are part of commercial diplomacy and are needed in Saudi Arabia, for example, as much as or more than in China.

Schmoozing with a long spoon is perfectly sensible and we should do more of it, not less. China is not an enemy, though some seem determined to make it one.

The Lone Ranger and the Posse

In the United States, and increasingly elsewhere, China is being portrayed as an enemy to be pursued by brave vigilantes. I would call this the LONE RANGER strategy.

At present there are two aspects to the strategy. The first is President Trump's highly idiosyncratic 'trade war' based on narrowing the bilateral deficit in goods. As discussed earlier, this makes no economic sense and, to the extent that it has any significant impact, imposes a cost on American consumers and China's other trade partners in order to generate a 'win' for President Trump in political terms.

Such political games have the merit of causing relatively little damage, especially as the Chinese appear to understand the game and seem inclined to make token concessions to help the President politically.

The second element, which is altogether more serious, is the attempt to exclude Chinese firms from key networks in order to maintain a US hegemony or to prevent Chinese companies from playing a lead role in them. Kicking out Huawei from the US is the most radical step so far, hindering Huawei's leadership in 5G technology. It is possible that the sanctions will harm Huawei sufficiently to stop its progress in 5G and create space for a US or European competitor to grow and to dominate telecommunications networks. It is more likely that China will accelerate indigenous development of the most

83

advanced semiconductors and that Huawei will continue to dominate global 5G but with less involvement of non-Chinese suppliers.

The strategy isn't just about Huawei and technology and trade. It is also about trying to decouple America's financial and business links with China. There are moves, so far threatened rather than acted upon, to make it difficult or even impossible for Chinese multinational firms to access American exchanges and capital markets and for American investors to access Chinese markets. So far the appetite of American financial institutions for Chinese money has frustrated the US authorities. And the Chinese are responding by welcoming more economic integration. But that may change leading to a more fragmented world.

The Lone Ranger style may suit President Trump but more thoughtful American officials and opposition Democrats have mooted the idea of a 'broad alliance': what could be called a POSSE.

We can see already the formation of a Posse in the overlap in language and action between the USA and its closest allies-the UK and Australia- and other countries which have separate quarrels with China- notably India. Some Far Eastern countries have reason to fear China and, in varying degrees, rely on US protection, like Japan, South Korea and Taiwan. It also seems likely that, when President Trump moves on, it will be politically easier for other countries to join the posse: Germany, France, Canada.

But what would the posse be for? In the case of the NATO alliance against the Soviet Union's Warsaw pact, there was a clear rationale: a strong, well-armed, military adversary, occupying large parts of Europe. There was a common interest in defence and deterrence reinforced by ideological glue.

China is not in the same position, having a deeply inferior and largely defensive military capability and no 'empire' outside what it regards as China. Its strengths are economic; it is not 'Upper Volta with rockets'. As for the ideological glue, modern China is authoritarian, as are quite a few of its adversaries, but it is also uncompromisingly capitalist, whatever the 'Communist' label.

Apart from incoherence, the dangers of the Posse approach are obvious. The first is that, fearing encirclement, China becomes even more nationalistic in tone and aggressive in behaviour. It would form even closer alliances with Russia and other anti-Western governments. In a more polarised world, localised disputes become global with Europe drawn in to disturb the delicate balance of forces in East Asia or the US drawn actively into the conflicts of the Indian subcontinent. Cold wars can become hot.

A second likely consequence is that China's economic and technological progress continues largely unhindered but increasingly the world becomes divided into rival systems and standards with little attention to overarching global problems like climate change or multilateral trade rules.

The Merkel Model

For these reasons I believe the only sensible approach is what I call the MERKEL MODEL.

Individual schmoozing-with a long spoon- should go along with a collective approach amongst likeminded countries to engage with China.

There are several areas where this really matters.

First, many of the points of friction with China on economic matters can and should be handled through the WTO: trade barriers, subsidies to 'state capitalist' enterprises, intellectual property rights, export and ownership restrictions. If the USA, EU, Japan, Canada and others had a common agenda and tactical coordination and a willingness to act collectively to enforce WTO rulings, it would be more effective than random, bilateral, squabbles. We know that China values its WTO membership and recognises that both its interests and image would be enhanced by acquiring the status of a 'market economy'.

China was promised progress to Market Economy Status by 2016, and it has been withheld, it claims illegally. China's trade partners have a juicy carrot as well as sticks to get China to behave in trade like the developed economy it now claims to be.

A second area of potential common ground is international economic coordination and finance. China has legitimate aspirations to be treated on rough parity with the USA in the IMF and World Bank and to make a commensurate contribution to their resources. At the beginning of the last decade, China made a big contribution to global recovery (though no doubt for self-interested reasons) and it remains a crucial contributor to global economic governance through the G20 as well as the Bretton Woods institutions.

A key, positive, step in future will be if, following the liberalisation of capital movements in 2015 and acceptance of the renminbi in the basket of currencies which make up the SDR (Special Drawing Rights), China were encouraged to move further to capital account liberalisation and convertibility, which would entail further economic liberalisation.

A third issue is humanitarian. Africa faces an acute post-Covid economic crisis in the wake of collapsing commodity export and tourist markets. The crisis is leading to massive poverty and hardship. There is a broad consensus that one contribution creditor nations can make is to write off official, government, debt. China accounts for roughly a half. Western creditors will baulk at debt write-offs if it is merely helping African countries service their debts to China (and vice versa): hence the need for a coordinated approach.

A crucial fourth is climate change. At present China earns a lot of Brownie points by subscribing to international agreements to curb emissions, unlike the USA. But it is the world's largest emitter of carbon, its emissions are growing and a programme of new coal-powered power stations shows lack of seriousness. Were a new American President persuaded to join the negotiating process it would possible, with the EU and the UK, to press China for serious commitments and deployment of its undoubted capability in solar, wind and nuclear.

The most immediate challenge internationally is the continued Covid crisis and beyond that are future pandemics. We can have a historical debate about whether China's initial cover-up was more culpable than the negligence of governments in major countries like the USA and Brazil. But, in future, it is essential that there is close cooperation with China, within a WHO framework, over the sharing of data and research and the avoidance of vaccine nationalism.

Little of this can be accomplished in a new Cold War. It will be difficult in any event. Critics of China point to its selective approach to the implementation of legally binding international agreements. It can in turn point fingers at Western countries which are also cavalier in their respect for such agreements, the UK being a particular offender at present in relation to Brexit. And the United States under Trump will even not engage in the multilateral process at all (Climate; WTO; WHO).

But if we were to get to the starting line, with governments agreeing that they have no alternative but to cooperate on shared problems, we still have the problem of Western politicians, in and out of government, determined to distance themselves from countries which do not follow their democratic model and definition of human rights.

Putting aside the inconsistency and shallowness of much of the current Western virtue signalling, there is the simple political reality that China has no intention of changing its political system, especially under external pressure. That is why I have called my approach the Merkel Model since she, unlike the more ideological Western leaders, has demonstrated high ethical standards and uncompromising commitment to democracy, but grounded in political and economic reality. Without such principled pragmatism, the prospects are very grim.

Selected References

There is a vast literature on modern China. The references below are especially useful.

Graham Allison *Destined for War; can America and China Escape the Thucydides Trap?* Scribe, London, 2018

Jung Chang and Jon Halliday *Mao: the Unknown Story* Jonathan Cape, 2005

Duncan Clarke *Alibaba: the House that Jack Built* Harper Collins, 2016

Bob Davis and Lingling Wei *Superpower Showdown* Harper Collins, 2020

Martin Jacques *When China Rules the World* Allen Lane, 2009

William Joseph *Politics in China: an Introduction* OUP, 2019

Matthew Klein and Michael Pettis *Trade Wars and Class Wars* Yale UP, 2020

Kishore Mahbubani *Has China Won?* Public Affairs 2020

Barry Naughton *The Chinese Economy: Transitions and Growth* MIT 2007

Margaret Roberts *Censored; Distraction and Diversion Inside China's Great Firewall* Princeton UP 2018

Edward Tse *Chinese Disrupters* London Printbooks, Penguin 2016

Ezra Vogel *Deng Xiaoping and the Transformation of China* Harvard UP 2011

Denis Wang *Reigning the Future: AI, 5G, Huawei and the Next 30 Years of US-China Rivalry* New Degree Press 2020

Jonathan Watts *When a Billion Chinese Jump* Faber and Faber 2010

Bite-Sized Public Affairs Books

Bite-Sized Public Affairs Books are designed to provide insights and stimulating ideas that affect us all in, for example, journalism, social policy, education, government and politics.

They are deliberately short, easy to read, and authoritative books written by people who are either on the front line or who are informed observers. They are designed to stimulate discussion, thought and innovation in all areas of public affairs. They are all firmly based on personal experience and direct involvement and engagement.

The most successful people all share an ability to focus on what really matters, keeping things simple and understandable. When we are faced with a new challenge most of us need quick guidance on what matters most, from people who have been there before and who can show us where to start.

They can be read straight through at one easy sitting and then referred to as necessary – a trusted repository of hard-won experience.

Bite-Sized Books Catalogue

We publish Business Books, Life-Style Books, Public Affairs Books, including our Brexit Books, Fiction – both short form and long form – and Children's Fiction.

To see our full range of books, please go to

https://bite-sizedbooks.com/

Printed in Great Britain
by Amazon